A MARRIAGE
OF TRUE MINDS

A MARRIAGE OF TRUE MINDS

AN INTIMATE PORTRAIT OF LEONARD AND VIRGINIA WOOLF

GEORGE SPATER
AND
IAN PARSONS

HARCOURT BRACE JOVANOVICH
NEW YORK AND LONDON

To Trekkie

who made this book possible

LC 77-73062

ISBN 0-15-157449-9

First American edition 1977
B C D E

Set in Great Britain by Cox & Wyman Ltd
Printed in Great Britain by Jolly & Barber Ltd, Rugby

CONTENTS

ILLUSTRATIONS

ACKNOWLEDGMENTS

Two monumental works dealing with the lives of Leonard and Virginia Woolf have been published since 1960: the five volumes of autobiography written by Leonard Woolf and the two-volume biography of Virginia Woolf written by her nephew Quentin Bell.

Since then, a significant amount of new material, which broadens our knowledge of the two principals, has become accessible. In 1972 the Berg Collection of the New York Public Library acquired a large archive including eighty-four letters from Lytton Strachey to Leonard Woolf which had hitherto been thought lost. Several of these letters throw added light on the efforts made by Strachey to promote a marriage between Leonard and Virginia (chapter 4). The archive purchased by the Berg also included one of the few extant letters written by Leonard to Virginia during their courtship (chapter 5). The first three volumes of *The Letters of Virginia Woolf*, edited by Nigel Nicolson, published in 1975–7, have been drawn upon extensively throughout the present work, and Nicolson's *Portrait of a Marriage*, published in 1973, provides valuable insights into Vita Sackville-West and her relations with Virginia Woolf (chapters 8 and 9). The massive Woolf archive, consisting of an estimated 60,000 letters and documents, which through the generosity of Trekkie Parsons passed to the University of Sussex in 1969, has only recently been sorted and classified. It contains Leonard's Ceylon account book (chapter 4), the original records of The Hogarth Press (chapter 7), an 1898 diary of Leonard Woolf (chapter 1), fifteen unpublished letters from Katherine Mansfield to Virginia Woolf (chapter 9) and much else of interest. The authors of the present work have also had access to the personal diaries of Leonard Woolf covering a period of sixty years, from 1910 to 1969. These diaries and other documents have made it possible to correct a number of the errors that appear in the five volumes of Leonard Woolf's autobiography, written largely when the author was in his eighties. Several of the errors have been specifically identified in the text, but in a number of other instances the correct data have been given here without comment. Where differences occur between the current work and the autobiography, the authors have satisfied themselves about the accuracy of the information they have used.

Finally, the authors have been fortunate in being allowed to make full use of the photographs in the five Monks House albums now in the possession of Mrs Parsons. These, with the Stella Duckworth album at the Berg, have made it possible to provide well over 100 photographs which have not previously appeared in any publication.

It is not possible to venture into the world of the Woolfs without becoming a debtor of Professor Quentin Bell, whose magnificent full-length biography of Virginia Woolf and his earlier *Bloomsbury* (1968) are, and must remain, classic works in this field. We have, additionally, a special debt of gratitude to Professor and Mrs Bell for answering questions as they arose, for reading our book in manuscript, and for offering helpful suggestions which, we trust, have been adequately reflected in the printed volume. We are indebted also to Mrs Parsons for the loan of Leonard Woolf's personal diaries and to Paul Levy for reading a draft of chapter 2.

Others to whom we are indebted for the use of copyright matter are Mrs Angelica Garnett (for Virginia Woolf and Vanessa Bell); Mrs. Middleton Murry, the Society of Authors as agent for the estate of Katherine Mansfield and as agent for the Strachey Trust; Michael Holroyd, author of the biography of Lytton Strachey; A. D. Peters as agent for Alec Waugh, for permission to quote from a letter; King's College, Cambridge, for permission to quote from a letter from E. M. Forster, and Mme Catherine Guillaume for the extract from Richard Aldington's letter, and Mrs Valerie Eliot for the letter in verse by T. S. Eliot. All other copyright sources are, we hope, identified and acknowledged in the *References* on pp. 191-205.

Lastly we wish to thank Peter Lewis, Librarian, and Adrian Peasgood, sub-Librarian, of the University of Sussex, for facilitating the use of materials in the possession of the University library.

G.S.

I.M.P.

INTRODUCTION

'I am very happy to have been invited to read and to write about this book.' I wonder how many hundreds of thousands of times those words have been used without the least tincture of sincerity. But not on this occasion: for George Spater and Ian Parsons have written a work on Virginia Woolf which makes a real and important contribution to our knowledge, a book which not only tells us things that are new, things which result obviously from an extensive and intelligent research involving the use of hitherto untapped sources, but also things which are important in themselves. The subject is one in which we need all the help that we can get, and these authors really are extraordinarily helpful. Moreover all this has been accomplished in a clear and lucid way without affectation or 'fine writing'.

Nor is this all, for they join to the study of Virginia a study of Leonard, and this also is rich in new material. Here, admittedly, their task was easier because they were entering upon a less thoroughly exploited territory; but the results are not for that reason any the less interesting. And I must not forget to mention, not I must admit without some degree of envy, that they have been outrageously fortunate in discovering new photographic sources, a form of historical documentation which is surely extremely important.

Books such as this, that is to say genuine and serious historical studies, are what I had always hoped would result from my own work. When, about twelve years ago, Leonard Woolf asked me to write the 'official biography' of Virginia, I had considerable doubts as to whether I ought to undertake such a task, and one of the things which in the end decided me to do so was precisely that my work would provide the basis upon which studies like *A Marriage of True Minds* would be undertaken; the book, or rather the idea of books such as this was, in a sense, the raison d'être of mine.

At the risk of being pompous and boring I should like to discuss some of the misgivings which I had to contend with when I was deciding whether to accept Leonard's very generous proposal and why it was that, in the end, I did decide to make the attempt. If I can find a way of expressing myself properly on this subject I may also succeed in saying why it is that I consider this new book so valuable.

Already, in 1964, there was a considerable body of literature devoted to the study of Virginia Woolf. But it fell into two very unequal parts. On the one hand there was Aileen Pippett's *The Moth and the Star*, which was in effect a 'Life' of Virginia. On the other hand there were a good many critical studies devoted to a discussion of her work. The division between these two categories was anything but tidy; Aileen Pippett adorned her tale with a discussion of the novels; the critics often supplied a brief account of the novelist's life. And in fact it was this, though not this alone, which worried me. It seemed that the biographer was expected to be a critic and the critic a biographer, and although I believed that I might write a passable account of Virginia's life I had very serious doubts as to whether I could say anything new or at all interesting about her novels. To say anything new was indeed the most frightening proposition; for to do so it would clearly be necessary to read all that had been written about them by others and this, I must confess, appeared to me an impossibly heroic undertaking.

In the end it seemed that the story of Virginia's life was so remarkable that it might stand by itself and that it would gain nothing, or less than nothing, from a recapitulation by me of that which had been said of her work by others, or by an assessment of that which every intelligent or sensitive reader had better assess for himself. For this I have been taken to task by Mr Spater's compatriots; but they have in other respects been so indulgent that I felt, or rather I have continued to feel, that for me at all events this was the only sensible decision. Sensible, yes; but also, I must admit, cowardly. If I had had more confidence in my own powers I might have made the attempt. I should like to be able to produce literary criticism, just as I should like to produce a great novel or a great poem, but it appears to me a task equally, if not more, difficult.

As I have said, when I began to write the life of Virginia Woolf my hope was that I should open the way for others, as Michael Holroyd's life of Strachey had opened the way for me, to make further contributions to a department of cultural history which had not been adequately examined. In it I tried to tell the truth: George Spater and Ian Parsons have done likewise. And for this, the present moment seems propitious. There are still a great many witnesses able to provide evidence; the archives at my disposal were extensive, but there was plenty of room left for others who wanted to research in this field. And, since I wrote, further evidence has become available. The opportunity for a study such as this one seems large. That such studies are needed I am sure. In an area of history such as this, no one can 'do' a subject. The story of Virginia and Leonard is something many-faceted, elusive, susceptible to many different kinds of explanation. It is altogether right and useful that the work of a biographer who comes to his task with the insights, but also with the prejudices, of a nephew should be supplemented by those who come from different backgrounds and in one case from another hemisphere. History is something too complex to be written by any one person, it is built—or at least one hopes that it will be built—by historians who approach the facts from different points of the compass and are united only by a common interest and a common integrity.

Up till now, I must admit, my expectations had not been completely realised. The Official Life has been followed by a spate of Lupine studies but these have in the main been critical rather than factual, while the search for truth, in so far as it has been pursued, has rather tended to be either frivolous or salacious (let me confess, horrible though it may be to do so, that I would rather read almost any frivolous and salacious journalism than almost any literary criticism). These works are the by-products of what is, in the academic world, a growth industry, and have attained such a volume that, in the Preface to an exhibition devoted to Bloomsbury, I was moved to make the following inquiry: 'Haven't you had enough?'

The answer, so far as serious historical studies are concerned, appears to me to be: 'No.' By this I do not mean that the public is not yet satiated; for all I know it may be bored to tears, although I doubt it. What I do mean is that it needs further instruction. There is still ignorance enough to justify a work such as *A Marriage of True Minds* a hundred times over. The sad thing, from my point of view, is that the efforts that have been made to try and provide some elementary facts about Bloomsbury have not been sufficient to check even the wildest varieties of myth and muddle. To do that, what we need is someone intelligent and honest, someone able to check and cross-examine the evidence, someone able to look with new eyes at old generalisations, to examine account books, to search for new visual evidence, to probe the arcana of those mysterious beings the Apostles, to bring our rapidly growing knowledge up to date and to furnish an authoritative and readable summary. In fact, what we need is this book.

QUENTIN BELL

January 1977

1 *Leonard's father, Sidney Woolf, a Q.C. at a time when there were only 175 in all England and* **2** *his mother, Marie Woolf, at 84. She was, according to Virginia, 'as spry as a weasel'. She lived to be 91*

[I]

THE EARLY YEARS

There were nine children in the Woolf home in Kensington. A tenth child died in infancy. Bella, the eldest, was born in 1877, and nearly every year thereafter until 1889 another child was added to the nursery: Herbert 1879, Leonard 1880, Harold 1882, Edgar 1883, Clara 1885, Flora 1886, Cecil 1887 and Philip 1889. The house at 101 Lexham Gardens was a large one:

'The servants' (there were eight of them and a governess) worked in and lived in the extremities; in the basement they did their work and there the footman had an underground bedroom; high up at the top in an area to which we never penetrated the female servants slept. Below this area were the two nurseries and the two nurses with the nursery children; on the floor below this lived the elder children who had been promoted to the life of the school-room; and below this again on the first floor and ground floor were my father and mother ...

The father of this small city was Sidney Woolf—a barrister—a Q.C. with 'an eager and a nipping air' and an income of £5,000 a year, who was driven in his own brougham every morning to King's Bench Walk. Sidney Woolf, 'very nervous and highly strung', whose intellectual intolerance, according to his son Leonard, 'seemed to be roughly proportionate to his ethical tolerance', came from a large Jewish family distinguished for its 'toughness and sternness'. The mother, Marie Woolf, was born in Holland of Jewish parents named de Jongh* who migrated to London when she was a child. The de Jonghs, also a large family, although physically tough were psychologically soft. 'I loved your mother', wrote one of Leonard's cousins, 'but I was afraid of your father.'

Leonard admired his father enormously. For a long while it was assumed that he would follow his father's profession. 'I think he was both fond and proud of me, because as a small boy I was intelligent, reserved, and had a violent temper, and so in fact resembled him.' Leonard resembled his father in other respects. He inherited his father's nervous tremor of the hands, and his intellectual intolerance. And as Leonard himself modestly expressed it 'from my very early years I have had in me, I think, a streak of considerable obstinacy'. This was a characteristic that lasted a lifetime. 'The main outlines of one's charac-ter', wrote Leonard, 'are moulded in infancy and do not change be-tween the ages of three and eighty-three.' At a *New Statesman* board meeting when he was in his eighties Leonard made an extremely serious charge against one of the *New Statesman* employees. The employee was immediately able to refute the charge by written documents, and demanded an apology. All the other directors agreed that an apology was in order. Leonard simply sat still, shaking, saying nothing, then slowly explained that ever since he was a boy he had never apologised regardless of circumstances, and that he could not do so now. He was asked, alter-natively, to withdraw the charge he had made. After a long wait he said he would withdraw it—'reluctantly'.

* Leonard's mother is described in his birth certificate as 'Marie Woolf, late Goldstucker formerly de Jongh'. Her father, Nathan Jacob de Jongh was not 'knocked down and killed . . . by a horse-drawn omnibus' as stated in Leonard's autobiography (1 LW 20) but hurt himself when he accidentally slipped off a kerb.

It is not difficult to understand how Edgar, who was not his father's favourite, might have found his older brother overbearing, as he did. Yet despite whatever sibling rivalry may have existed under the surface, or even in occasional outbreaks above it, the Woolfs were a cheerful and happy family. The parents were kind to their children—they rarely punished them—and the children found their pleasures largely within the household and the homes of their many relations, who possibly were not fully aware of the interest the Woolf children took in them: a favourite card game was played with photographs of their numerous aunts and uncles in which the ugliest took the trick. There was a family newspaper known as the *Z.N.*—the *Zoological News*—published in thirty-three numbers from 1897 to 1900, to which Leonard was an occasional contributor, but which was chiefly the work of the younger children in the family. Every year the family was carried off for a holiday in the country: to Henley, Tenby, Penmaenmawr, Speldhurst, Whitby. 'When the day came, six, seven, eight, and eventually nine children, servants, dogs, cats, canaries, and at one time two white rats in a bird cage, mountains of luggage were transported in an omnibus to the station and then in a reserved "saloon" railway carriage to our destination.'

Life in this style ended in 1892 when Sidney Woolf died at the early age of 48, leaving his widow and nine children—the eldest 16, the youngest 3–with insufficient capital to live as they had in the past. Servants were released, the large house was sold, and the survivors— including a cook, parlourmaid and housemaid—moved to a small house in Colinette Road, Putney.

While Sidney Woolf was alive, the children were taught mostly by nurses, governesses and tutors at home. Herbert, at 12, had been sent to Arlington House, Brighton, and each of the other sons, when about the same age, went to the same school, enabled to do so by the generosity of the headmaster who accepted them at greatly reduced fees. At Arlington House Leonard learned to play cricket with 'style' from one of the masters, and about sex from a 'small boy who had probably the dirtiest mind in an extraordinarily dirty-minded school'. Leonard's previous association with sex had been limited to kindergarten experiences: 'I habitually sat illicitly holding under the table the hand of a small yellow-haired girl, and . . . I somehow or other induced a rather older girl, with black hair, who was not in the kindergarten, to cause an open scandal by kissing me in the hall.'

In 1894 Leonard won a scholarship to St Paul's School, as did three of his younger brothers: Edgar, Cecil and Philip. The High Master of St

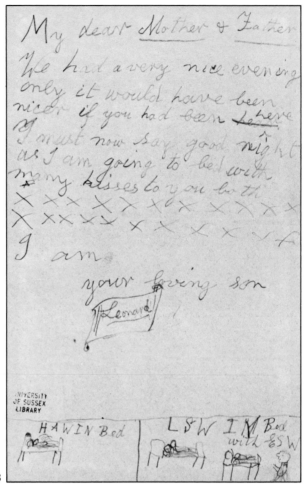

3

3 *In this letter to his parents, Leonard has portrayed the sleeping arrangements for his older brother Herbert (HAW), for himself (LSW), and for his younger brother Edgar (ESW) who, 70 years later, complained of Leonard's bullying*

4 *Letter from Leonard to his father, May 27, 1890*

5 *The Leonard Paper, August 4, 1889. Several years before the Stephen children began publishing the* Hyde Park Gate News, *an 8-year-old Leonard Woolf was producing what seems to be his first journalistic effort in a career that continued for 80 years.*

FORCAST. This morning it was the most loveliest morning you could wish for the sun was shining beautifully.

MAMA. At the beginning of the day Mrs Woolf had a bad headack.

EXCHANGE. Wanted a bunch of flowers a piece of swand paper in exchange.

EXERDANTS. Great Exerdants with a cat wich fell down and broke its legs.

SAD DISAPPOINTMENT IN THE WOOLFS DEN. A gentleman was expected for dinner but did not come. End.

101 Lexham Gdns
27 May 1890

My darling Papa

I hope you are quite well & that you are enjoying yourself. We went to meet Uncle John & Aunt Jenny & they seemed quite well. I suppose you heard

from Herbert that a cat got into the garden under the wire. We saw a very funny sight yesterday just as we were going into High Street we saw a fourwheeler with four men inside one on the box & two on the roof.

Another curious thing happened in our garden a butterfly settled on the grass but a sparrow pounced upon it & took it away leaving one wing on the grass.

I must now say good bye as I am going to do my lessons for Mister Floyd with much love

I remain
Your loving son
Leonard.

The Leonard Paper.
Aug't 4, 1889.

Forcast.

This morning it was the most loveliest morning you could wish for the Sun was shining beautifully

Mama

At the beginning of the day Mrs Woolf had a bad head ach.

Exchange

Wanted a bunch of flowers a

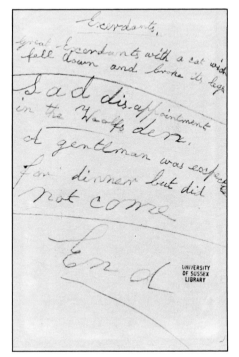

Ecirdants.

Great Ecirdants with a cat who fell down and broke its leg.

Sad disappointment in the Woolfs den.

A gentleman was expected for dinner but did not come.

En

6 *Leonard at Studland in 1911 with his eldest sister, Bella, and Mrs Ross, a Woolf neighbour, whose daughter married Edgar Woolf, Leonard's brother*

7 *Leonard's mother and his eldest sister, Bella*

Paul's at that date was F. W. Walker, who year after year during Leonard's time was able to report that Paulines had won more scholarships than Eton, Harrow, Winchester, Rugby or any of the other famous public schools of England. 'It is he', writes G. K. Chesterton, 'of whom the famous tale is told that, when a fastidious lady wrote to ask him what was the social standing of the boys at his school, he replied, "Madam, so long as your son behaves himself and the fees are paid, no questions will be asked about his social standing".' Leonard was a great success at St Paul's. He played cricket, football and fives. He also had a distinguished scholastic record, winning a host of Pauline prizes as well as an exhibition and sub-sizarship to Trinity College, Cambridge. What is even more impressive, he learnt the classics so thoroughly that he was able to read Latin and Greek with ease throughout his life. 'Clever and should do well' was Walker's laconic assessment in 1898. As Leonard himself put it: 'I was lamentably intelligent . . . a horrid little intellectual.'

During his last year at St Paul's Leonard was elected to the Junior Debating Society (there was no senior debating society) an exclusive group of exceptionally talented boys who met on Saturday afternoons at the houses of the members. Chesterton, six years senior to Leonard, was one of the members and was still a regular attendant at the meetings. They were an important prelude to Leonard's years at Cambridge.

While Leonard was at St Paul's his sister Bella had begun to earn money by writing for magazines. A book containing one of her short stories was published in 1894, when she was only 17, and two children's books written by her appeared in 1897 and 1898. Herbert, a year older than Leonard, left school for the City and a career on the Stock Exchange. Edgar, Cecil and Philip followed Leonard to Cambridge; Cecil as an exhibitioner of Trinity College and the other two as scholars of Sidney Sussex College. But Marie Woolf held her family tightly together. Bella and Herbert as well as the seven younger children continued to live at home. Only from Leonard came signs of rebellion. 'She loved all her nine surviving children', wrote Leonard in his autobiography, 'but she loved me less, I think, than any of the eight others, because she felt me to be unsympathetic to her view of the family, of the universe, and of the relation of the one to the other.' No further explanation is offered, but at a later point Leonard said, 'I know that it was not long after my fourteenth birthday* that I announced that I was an unbeliever and would not in

* Leonard was mistaken about the date this occurred, since his diary entry for September 26, 1898 (when he was nearly 18) reads 'Went synagogue all day'. No diaries exist for the years 1899–1904.

future go to synagogue, and I am sure that I had been contemplating this step for some time before I took it.* When I solemnly announced to my mother that I no longer believed in Jehovah she wept, but her tears were not very convincing, I think, either to me or to her. She was genuinely distressed, but not very acutely; that I should repudiate the deity and refuse to go to synagogue caused a family sensation, but only a mild one which lasted a very short time.'

Almost certainly there were other manifestations of lack of sympathy on Leonard's part. For one thing, he thought his mother cried too much. In his description of her in *The Wise Virgins*, his second novel, published in 1914, he mentioned her tears, and pictured her as grotesquely over-dressed, addicted to constant small talk, and peevish. The other children frequently referred to their mother as 'Lady'. Leonard never did. When Leonard was married to Virginia Stephen his mother was outraged by their refusal to invite her to the wedding. None of Leonard's brothers or sisters attended. There was no open breach, but from time to time they forthrightly told Leonard that he unfairly failed to give credit to their widowed mother for her intelligence and fortitude in single-handedly bringing up a large family. These protestations brought about no change in Leonard's attitude. Yet he regularly called on his mother every two or three weeks until her death in 1939.

Leonard reported other changes in his life that took place while he was at St Paul's. He developed, so he asserted, a façade or carapace 'as a protection to the naked, tender, shivering soul', a device to hide his real feelings from the 'outside and usually hostile world'. This façade 'as the years went past, grew ever thicker and more elaborate'. And thus, by 1899, he was prepared for University life with a sound classical foundation acquired at St Paul's, a scholarship that covered most of his expenses, a hard shell to protect himself against an unfriendly universe, a firm belief in his own intelligence, and a newly found freedom from the trammels of any established religion.

Virginia Stephen was born on January 25, 1882, at 22 Hyde Park Gate, Kensington, five minutes by horse-drawn carriage from the Woolf residence in Lexham Gardens. The two families had the same physician —a Dr Seton—but otherwise may be said to have lived in different worlds. There were, in each case, the large Victorian house, the many servants, the large family, the summer holidays in the country. But 22 Hyde Park Gate had a cultural life of such breadth and intensity that it necessarily affected its occupants as few other London houses could have done. To it came the leaders of art and intellect: painters, art critics, ambassadors, statesmen, civil servants, judges, philosophers, distinguished academics, poets, novelists, publishers and journalists.

Virginia's father, Leslie Stephen (he was made K.C.B. in 1902), was the son of Sir James Stephen, Colonial Under-Secretary, and grandson of James Stephen, a Master in Chancery. All three were writers. Sir Leslie was an essayist, critic, editor, biographer, philosopher-historian. His *History of English Thought in the Eighteenth Century*, published in 1876, six years before Virginia was born, was an instant success and a century later is still in print. Leslie Stephen was the first editor of the *Dictionary of National Biography*, a work of monumental scholarship, for it recaptured the lives of the great men of English history 'from the earliest times' and placed them in perspective to each other. He was editor of the *Cornhill* for eleven years. He wrote seven separate biographies (in addition to the 378 he wrote for the *DNB*) including the inaugural volume—on Samuel Johnson—in the *English Men of Letters* series. He was selected in preference to Gladstone to succeed Tennyson as President of the London Library, and was given honorary degrees by Oxford, Cambridge, Edinburgh and Harvard. When he was a student at Cambridge he was an outstanding runner and oarsman, and later he became famous as a mountain climber; but he had been delicate and sickly as a child, fragile looking, easily fatigued and exhausted—almost an invalid. He was also shy, and painfully sensitive to criticism. When he was three years old his mother wrote: 'A word or even a look of blame puts him into an agony of distress', and two years later: 'He is the most sensitive child I ever saw.'*

Virginia's mother—the beautiful Julia Jackson—came from another distinguished family, but one of different distinctions. Her father and two of her uncles had served in India in important civilian capacities. Her aunt Virginia was Countess Somers, mother of the Duchess of Bedford. Another aunt was Julia Margaret Cameron, pioneer English photographer. Still another was Sarah Prinsep, friend of writers and painters.

Julia Jackson's first husband was Herbert Duckworth, who died in 1870 leaving her (she was only 24) with three babies: George, Stella and Gerald. Virginia's father, too, had been married before, to Harriet Marian Thackeray, daughter of the novelist; she had died in 1875. They had had one child: a mentally retarded girl, Laura. Thus when Leslie Stephen married Julia Jackson Duckworth in 1878 they began with a

---

* A sensitivity he never lost: 'I am, like my father,' Leslie Stephen wrote in 1895, '"skinless", over-sensitive and nervously irritable.'

household of four children, and quickly added four more: Vanessa in 1879, Thoby 1880, Virginia 1882 and Adrian 1883.

The house at 22 Hyde Park Gate, a rather dreary structure of five storeys, was enlarged to seven in order to hold the expanded family and the numerous servants that were necessary in Victorian times for a family of that size. The four small Stephen children occupying the two nurseries at the top of the house comprised a distinct unit, since they were roughly ten years younger than the four children of the prior marriages. Adrian was always regarded as the baby (he was his mother's favourite) and a strong alliance that lasted all their lives was formed between Vanessa, Thoby and Virginia: Vanessa serene and practical; Thoby fair-minded, handsome and vigorous; Virginia wild and impish. Virginia not only had a keen sense of the comic—she was frequently convulsed with laughter—but discovered very early that she had the power of provoking laughter in others, seizing upon some random fact and building it into an elaborate fantasy through her free-flowing imagination. Her listeners might be enthralled, shocked or amused, depending on their sensibilities and the extent to which the story departed from reality.

At an early date it was apparent that Vanessa was to be a painter; her father drew well and often entertained his children with his sketches of animals, while several of the outstanding English painters of the day, among them Watts, Burne-Jones and Holman Hunt, were friends of the family. It was equally apparent that Virginia was to be a writer, as her Stephen ancestors had been for 150 years. And what could be more natural than that a household that was on terms of familiarity with Thackeray, Tennyson, George Eliot, Meredith, Henry James and Thomas Hardy should produce a writer?

Virginia took to pen and ink 'as some people do to gin'. Her first vehicle was the *Hyde Park Gate News*, a weekly publication begun in 1891 as a joint enterprise with Thoby and Vanessa and continued, mainly through the exertions of Virginia, until 1895. Issue no. 45, vol. ii, dated November 21, 1892, contained this report written by Virginia, then aged ten:

Mr. Leslie Stephen whose immense literary powers are well known is now the President of the London Library which as Lord Tennyson was before him and Carlyle was before Tennyson is justly esteemed a great honour. Mrs. Ritchie the daughter of Thackeray who came to luncheon the next day expressed her delight by jumping from her chair and clapping her hands in a childish manner but none the less sincerely. The greater part of Mrs. Stephen's joy lies in the fact that Mr. Gladstone is only vice-president. She is not at all of a 'crowy' nature but we forgive any woman for triumphing when her husband gets above

8 *Leslie and Julia Stephen with Virginia in the background c. 1892*

9 *Virginia and Adrian Stephen c. 1886*

10 *Cricketers at St Ives c. 1892. At this period Virginia, ball in hand, was known in her family as the 'demon bowler'*

11

12

11 Front row: *Vanessa, Virginia, Adrian.* Back row: *Sir Leslie Stephen, Lady Albutt, Mrs Stephen, Gerald Duckworth, Sir C. Albutt. St Ives c. 1892*

12 Front row: *Stella Duckworth, Lily Norton, Vanessa, Virginia.* Back row: *Dick Norton, Julia Stephen with Adrian, Gratwick, Sir Leslie Stephen and Thoby*

13

14

13 *Thoby, Adrian, Vanessa and Virginia*

14 *Vanessa at her easel with Virginia, Thoby and Adrian*

15

16

15 *Adrian, Thoby, Vanessa and Virginia*

16 *George Duckworth and Virginia*

17 Front row: *Adrian, Mrs Stephen, Leslie Stephen*. Back row: *George Duckworth, Virginia, Thoby, Vanessa, Gerald Duckworth*

18 *Thoby Stephen with his father.* **19** *Thoby Stephen*

20

21

22

20 *Sophie Farrell, the family cook. When the second generation of Duckworths and Stephens found themselves separate living quarters she declared, 'I ought to be able to cut myself up among the lot of you'.* **21** *Help at St Ives c. 1892*

22 *Talland House as it looks today, converted into 'luxury holiday flats'. The top storey has been altered and a wing added at the right*

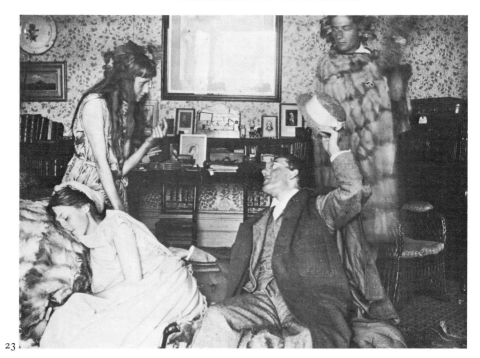

23 *Skylarking at St Ives, c. 1892* Standing: *Virginia and Jack Hills* Seated: *Vanessa and Walter Headlam.* **24** *Jack Hills and Stella Duckworth before they were married*

Mr. Gladstone. We think that the London Library has made a very good choice in putting Mr. Stephen before Mr. Gladstone as although Mr. Gladstone may be a first-rate politician he cannot beat Mr. Stephen in writing. But as Mr. Stephen with that delicacy and modesty which with many other good qualities is always eminent in the great man's manner went out of the room when the final debate was taking place we cannot oblige our readers with more of the interesting details.

Thus from their earliest days the younger Stephen children were familiar with notabilities, some at first hand, others through dinner-table conversation, and as befitted the offspring of their outspoken and heretical father, they regarded them with irreverent detachment. 'These great people', Virginia wrote in a typically impish tone, 'always talked much as you and I talk; Tennyson, for instance, would say to me, "Pass the salt" or "Thank you for the butter".' Crowds of bright young men gathered at Hyde Park Gate on Sundays when Julia Stephen held court. They came, as one admirer later recalled it, 'dressed in our best and longest frock coats and carrying (as the custom then was) our shiny hats into the drawing room. And I also remember a derisive and apparently hostile band of four, which haunted the back passage and used to mock at our self-conscious dignity.' The same hostile band delightedly, and hopefully, watched their father's friend Henry James when he tilted 'his chair perilously far back as he spun out the elaborate looped thread of his sentences. Once, the marvellous thing happened and he fell over backward, but finished his sentence on the floor.' This irreverence for the great was coupled with a religious irreverence of equal conviction inherited from their father, author of *An Agnostic's Apology* (1893). To their credit, however, the Stephen children – a true product of Victorian England – displayed proper embarrassment over the awkward presence of a French ancestor in their mother's family, four generations back.

From 1882 to 1894 summers were spent at St Ives in Cornwall, where the family rented Talland House, a large rambling structure overlooking the bay and the Godrevy Lighthouse. This was the scene of Virginia's happiest childhood recollections; the family was young and healthy and intact, Thoby and Adrian were home on holiday, there were all sorts of wonderful things to see and do, as Virginia relates in her novel *To the Lighthouse*. The Stephen children, according to a St Ives neighbour, 'were all tall and fair, never mixing with other children, almost like Gods and Goddesses'.

This idyll was destroyed in 1895 when Julia Stephen died. She was only 49 years old. Leslie Stephen was plunged into gloom. He had not only lost a deeply loved and loving wife, he had lost his own security;

for his happiness—his whole existence—had depended on the sympathy and the practical reassurance that for seventeen years his wife had given him. Virginia, a child of thirteen who had all her father's sensitivity, suffered a double loss of security: her mother was no longer there and her father, instead of providing support, became a drain on her sympathies and on those of the rest of the household. Again and again they saw the great man who had succeeded Tennyson and Carlyle, who had bested Gladstone, break down and cry at the dinner table. It was then that Virginia had her first mental breakdown. She heard 'voices', her pulse raced, she was excited and nervous. There is little to show to what extent it was thought serious at the time.* Like her father in his youth, Virginia had always been delicate. Dr Seton, who had been seeing Virginia since she was a baby, stopped her lessons and prescribed exercise.

After Julia Stephen's death her household duties, including the presentation of household accounts every Wednesday afternoon, were taken over by Stella Duckworth, and two years later, when Stella married, these duties devolved on Vanessa. Stella was so gloriously happy during her engagement that she brought cheer into what had been a household of unbroken gloom; but within three months of her marriage Stella too was dead. The stable world of pre-1895 St Ives began unfolding to a sensitive child as one of chaos in which, without warning, a devoted mother could die at 49 and a happy Stella could die at 28; while unhappy, unbalanced Laura lived on in asylums and nursing homes until she was 75. Virginia might well ponder the questions of life and love and death, and she had ample time to do it. For Virginia was desperately lonely. Her brothers, Thoby and Adrian, had been away at school since 1891-2. Her half-brothers, George and Gerald Duckworth, left the house daily to go to their work. Vanessa rode in the park in the morning and went off to art classes later in the day. When Vanessa 'came out' (she was three years older than Virginia) she was frequently away from the house in the evening. Virginia's own 'coming out' a few years later was a complete failure. She didn't know how to dress; she rejoiced in the informality of the country where 'there is very little need of clothing, which', Virginia commented, 'I always think a great point about Heaven'. She didn't have any small talk; at 22 Hyde Park Gate if you had nothing to say, you said nothing. 'I went to a dance last night', wrote Virginia, 'and found a dim corner where I sat and read In Memoriam.'

Because of her ill-health Virginia did not go riding with her sister, and

* Leonard incorrectly states that Virginia tried to commit suicide in the 1895 attack by jumping out of a window (3 LW 77). The incident occurred in 1904.

25 *Vanessa, taken in Rome, shortly after her marriage*

26

27

28

29

26-9 *These four remarkable photographs of Virginia alone, and with her father, were taken by G. C. Beresford around 1903. Although they have been occasionally reproduced, they have never been shown before as a group*

30   31

30 *Virginia*
31 *Virginia having breakfast at Brunswick Square where she lived in 1911–12*
32 *Janet Case, who taught Virginia Greek and remained a life-long friend, with Virginia and Vanessa in Firle Park c. 1911*

except for a few miscellaneous courses which she took at King's College London, did not go out of the house for her education. She was largely self-taught, with some help from her parents, and from tutors who came to Hyde Park Gate. Her exuberant imagination had not been dulled by academic discipline, and her natural sensitivity had not been blunted by association with less sensitive schoolfellows. Her scanty knowledge of sex, such as it was, had been acquired through classical literature, in contrast to the specifics imparted to Leonard by his youthful school-mate; she had been dismayed and embarrassed, rather than edified, by the clumsy erotic fumblings of her two Duckworth half-brothers. She was lonely too, as is confirmed by the frequency with which lonely characters appear in Virginia's novels. Much of the time during her adolescence Virginia was left alone in a seven-storey house with servants and a grieving father growing increasingly deaf, who shut himself in his study every morning, finding added cause for gloom in the loss of his closest friends, eight of whom died between 1896 and 1901. Henry James called 22 Hyde Park Gate 'that house of all the Deaths'.

In 1899 Thoby entered Trinity College, Cambridge. There he made many new friends. He joined a group of five other first-year students who called themselves the Midnight Society: Clive Bell, A. J. Robertson, Lytton Strachey, Saxon Sydney-Turner and Leonard Woolf. The group met in Clive Bell's rooms at midnight on Saturday for the purpose of reading poetry aloud.

Thoby's two beautiful sisters attended the Trinity May Week Ball in June 1900. There they met Thoby's lively friend Clive Bell who, although brought up on a regime of riding and hunting, was 'one of those strange Englishmen who break away from their environment and become devoted to art and letters'. The following summer they met Leonard Woolf when the two girls, chaperoned by their cousin Miss Katherine Stephen, Principal of Newnham College, came to Thoby's room 'in white dresses and large hats, with parasols in their hands. Their beauty', wrote Leonard years later, 'literally took one's breath away.'

Vanessa and Virginia were also very silent and to any superficial observer they might have seemed demure. Anyone who has ridden many different kinds of horses knows the horse who, when you go up to him for the first time, has superficially the most quiet and demure appearance, but, if after bitter experi-ence you are accustomed to take something more than a superficial glance at a strange mount, you observe at the back of the eye of this quiet beast a look which warns you to be very, very careful. So too the observant observer would have noticed at the back of the two Miss Stephens' eyes a look which would have warned him to be cautious, a look which belied the demureness, a look of great intelligence, hypercritical, sarcastic, satirical.

It is possible that Leonard read some of his later experiences into this vivid description of the Stephen girls.

[2]

THE APOSTLES

33 *Desmond MacCarthy and G. E. Moore at Monks House in the 1940s*

'It is necessary here', wrote Leonard Woolf in the first volume of his autobiography, 'to say something about the Society—The Apostles—because of the immense importance it had for us, its influence upon our minds, our friendships, our lives.' Although it is probable that Leonard's 'us' and 'our' referred to the Apostles themselves, it is also true that the influence of the Society on Virginia, while indirect, was of nearly equal importance in her own life.

Leonard was elected to the Society in 1902. At that time the other undergraduate members were Saxon Sydney-Turner (who shared rooms with Leonard in Great Court), Lytton Strachey, A. R. Ainsworth, Ralph Hawtrey, and J. T. Sheppard, later Provost of King's College. In the following year John Maynard Keynes was taken into the Society. Members previously elected who were still active in its affairs included E. M. Forster, Roger Fry, Desmond MacCarthy, Bertrand Russell, Alfred North Whitehead, Gerald Balfour, G. H. Hardy, G. M. Trevelyan and, most importantly, the philosopher G. E. Moore. Seven of these individuals: Woolf, Sydney-Turner, Strachey, Keynes, Forster, Fry and MacCarthy became part of what is now known as 'Bloomsbury'.

The formal name for the Apostles was The Cambridge Conversazione Society. It had been founded in 1820 as a secret association, but records that have become available on the death of its members reveal that some of the giants of the past included Alfred Tennyson, Arthur Hallam, James Clerk Maxwell, Henry Sidgwick and Richard Monckton Milnes (later Lord Houghton).

Members were selected with great discrimination. Although an average of less than three were added per year, Betrand Russell thought that the Society managed to attract 'most of the people of any intellectual eminence who have been at Cambridge', a statement that may possibly attest more to Russell's vanity than to his statistical accuracy, but containing nevertheless an element of truth. New undergraduates at Cambridge who had outstanding school records or had written distinguished entrance scholarship essays were singled out and observed at close range during their first year at the University. They were invited to teas and to walks where they met the members of the Society without, supposedly, knowing the purpose of the meetings. The individuals so observed were, in the jargon of the Society, 'embryos'.* Although sons, younger brothers and friends of Apostles were considered and their qualifications examined, such relationships provided no easy certificate of admission. Leslie Stephen, whose brother was a member of the Society, was not admitted and always regretted it. 'Let us hope', he said, 'that I learnt a lesson of humility.' Similar lessons of humility were meted out to Thoby and Adrian Stephen, sons of Sir Leslie. But his grandson Julian Bell, son of Vanessa Stephen and Clive Bell (a non-member), was elected to the Society about eighty years after his grandfather had failed. The rare candidate chosen for membership was 'born' when initiated. On initiation he was introduced to the 'ark', a cedar-wood chest, in which the documents of the Society were kept, including records of past proceedings, the registry signed by each of the members and one paper

---

* Sir Geoffrey Keynes, in *The Letters of Rupert Brooke* (1968) p. 145, incorrectly describes an embryo as one admitted to the Society.

by each member which had been read at a Society meeting.*

During term, meetings were held every Saturday night: 'for the active member attendance was a matter of honour and all other engagements had to give way'. Tea was served accompanied by anchovy toast, known as 'whales'. The members sat round the Society's hearth-rug while one, the 'moderator', read a paper which might be as short as fifteen minutes or as long as two hours. Discussion followed in which each of the others present was expected to take part, and the moderator was permitted to respond. Then a resolution was drafted (which often had no connection with the discussion) and the proposition voted on. Before breaking up, the subject of the paper to be read at the next meeting was settled by choosing between four titles, one usually humorous, submitted by the member who was to lead the discussion at that meeting. The discussions were primarily on literary or philosophical subjects. 'The social conditions did not seem quite so frightful or menacing before 1900 as they do today in retrospect ... It was the 1914 War that made people think as we do to-day,' Leonard later commented.

These regular meetings were not limited to the half-dozen or so undergraduate members, but were open to and attended by dons who were members and any other Apostle who happened to be in the vicinity. They, as well as the undergraduates, read papers and took part in the discussions that followed, including debates on the critical issue of which embryos were to be selected for admission. Members who had gone down and were no longer regularly present at the Saturday meetings 'took wings' and became 'angels'. The name 'Apostles' (which members of the Society allege was the creation of an 'envious and jeering' outsider otherwise unknown to history) presumably referred both to the numbers usually attending meetings and to the fact, according to Bertrand Russell, that 'We took ourselves perhaps rather seriously, for we considered that the virtue of intellectual honesty was in our keeping.'

This lofty feeling stemmed, no doubt, from the highly selective character of the Society and from its exalted objectives. The members of the Society were 'brothers' of Plato and other great philosophers; they lived in the World of Reality of the German metaphysicians and were therefore exempted from bondage to Space and Time. In contrast, non-members, referred to as 'phenomena', lived in a World of Appearances.

* Members present at the annual dinner of the Society on April 16, 1969, after discussing whether information 'about the early years of the Society ... might be made available to scholars' decided that 'at present ... no change would be made about the basic principle of secrecy'.

So too did the embryos.* This mumbo-jumbo was half humorous, half serious, but from the outset Leonard Woolf 'was one of the most apostolic men there have ever been, and he continued so to the very end of his long life'.

The Saturday evening discussions, according to Henry Sidgwick, were dominated by 'the spirit of the pursuit of truth with absolute devotion and unreserve by a group of intimate friends, who were perfectly frank with each other, and indulged in any amount of humorous sarcasm and playful banter, and yet each respects the other, and when he discourses tries to learn from him and see what he sees. Absolute candour was the only duty that the tradition of the society enforced. No consistency was demanded with opinions previously held—truth as we saw it then and there was what we had to embrace and maintain . . .' Bertrand Russell, writing seventy years later, confirmed Sidgwick's description: 'It was a principle in discussion that there were to be no *taboos*, no limitations, nothing considered shocking, no barriers to absolute freedom of speculation.'

In addition to the regular Saturday night meetings an annual dinner was held at a restaurant in London or, in the early days, at the 'Star and Garter' in Richmond. The President, an Angel, proposed a toast to the Society which was responded to by the Vice-President, the newest member of the Society. The President arranged for a series of toasts to be offered and responded to by other members present, which provided opportunities for the display of Apostolic wit and nostalgia. In 1922, when the economist Ralph Hawtrey, later Sir Ralph Hawtrey, was President, the toasts were:

> 'The Ark'
> 'The Whales'
> 'The Hearth-Rug'

This then, sketchily described, was the structure within which the Society operated. Three other elements are needed to explain the impact of the Society on its membership. First, the Society nearly always had its unnamed but universally regarded hero—usually one outside the Society itself. At an early date the hero was Barthold Niebuhr, the German historian who introduced modern scientific methods into the study of history. When Strachey, Woolf and Keynes were admitted into the Society, the hero was a member—G. E. Moore, fellow of Trinity College and later Professor of Philosophy.

---

* ' ... methinks we yet discourse in Platoes denne, and are but embryon Philosophers.'
Sir Thomas Browne, *Hydriotaphia* (1658) ch. IV.

34 *The announcement of the annual dinner in 1925 when Leonard was President*

The Cambridge Conversazione Society

Will dine at the

CONNAUGHT ROOMS, Great Queen Street,

On Tuesday, June 16th, 1925,

at 7.15 p.m.

Reply to

Leonard Woolf, 52 Tavistock Square, w.c.1

34

Cambridge Conversazione Society

Vins	MENU
	Melon Rafraichi
	or
	Hors d'Œuvre Variés
Sherry : Oloroso	Tortue Verte en Tasse
	Saumon Froid en Belle Vue Concombres
White Wine : Graves "Podensac"	
	Ris de Veau à la Crème
	Selle d'Agneau Sce. Menthe
Claret : Château Langoa Barton 1915	Petits Pois Nouveaux
	Pommes Nouvelles
	Pâté de Cailles Salvini
	Salade Romaine
Port : Delaforce Choice Old Reserve	
	Fraises Melba
	Petits Fours
	Café

The Connaught Rooms, Gt. Queen St., Kingsway.   June 16, 1925

35

36

---

35 *The seven course meal with four wines cost 20s. per person.*

36 *Seating arrangement in Leonard's hand for 32 members attending (out of total membership of 72): R. C. Trevelyan (Bob Trevy), Lytton Strachey (GLS), George Rylands, Roger Fry, James Parker Smith, A. L. Hobhouse, H. O. Meredith (HOM), R. B. Braithwaite, E. M. Forster, F. E. Harmer, G. Thomson, C. P. Sanger, J. M. Keynes, R. G. Hawtrey, A. P. D. Penrose, Edward H. Marsh, Frank D. Ramsey, F. L. Lucas, Frederick Pollock, A. H. Smith, G. L. Dickinson, Malcolm M. Macnaghten, G. M. Trevelyan, Robin Mayor, J. T. Sheppard, Lionel Penrose, James Strachey, Desmond MacCarthy, G. E. Moore, Austin Smythe, Saxon Sydney-Turner.*

In assessing Moore's influence on the generations of Cambridge men who studied under him, and on individuals like Virginia to whom Moore's ideas were indirectly transmitted, one must consider his method of argument as much as the substance of his conclusions. Moore concentrated on three things he considered essential: (1) determining and stating the question before attempting to answer it, (2) rejecting all received doctrine and opinion unless their 'truths' could be demonstrated, and (3) expressing thoughts simply and clearly. 'What exactly do you mean?' was the question repeatedly asked by Moore. These precepts, branded into the consciousness of his students by a variety of startling forensic devices (opening wide his eyes, raising his eyebrows, sticking out his tongue, wagging his head in the negative so violently that his hair shook), produced what Leonard Woolf referred to as the 'stringent' influence of Moore. 'It was this clarity, freshness, and common-sense which primarily appealed to us.' But Moore's extreme rationalism also appealed to his young disciples. Years later Leonard recognised that this had gone too far; that a religion based on precepts derived from Moore 'had two important defects ... It ignored the outside world of action, traditional wisdom, the restraints of custom, and those deep-seated emotions and instincts over which our predecessors, by means of that traditional wisdom, had built the thin precarious crust of civilisation. Closely allied to this defect was our worship of reason; we believed in the efficacy of reason as other religions had believed in the efficacy of prayer ... and what was even more disastrous, we attributed to human nature a rationality which it has never possessed. This pseudo-rational view gave both to thought and feeling a thinness and superficiality ... ' The consequence of these defects, stated succinctly by Roger Fry's daughter, was that 'some babies got thrown away with all that dirty bath-water they tipped out'.

Many of Moore's disciples also adopted his taciturnity, his unwillingness to say anything unless it was important to be said. When it was pointed out to him, half seriously and half humorously, that his own silence had silenced a generation, he replied, 'I didn't want to be silent, I couldn't think of anything to say.'

The final area of Moore's influence was derived from the substance of his teachings. Moore's *Principia Ethica*, published in 1903, became the bible to young Apostles of that period. The first four chapters of the book dealt with principles of ethical reasoning in which Moore described what he thought to be the fallacies in earlier writings on that subject. The two concluding chapters were 'Ethics in Relation to Conduct' and 'The Ideal'. The latter chapter contains the language which has been most frequently quoted by those discussing Moore's impact on his contemporaries: 'personal affections and aesthetic enjoyments include *all* the greatest, and *by far* the greatest, goods we can imagine'. These enjoyments are 'the *raison d'être* of virtue; ... they ... form the rational ultimate end of human action and the sole criterion of social progress'. *

Although Moore was not a homosexual himself, his words were used to justify homosexual relations; just as the even more famous pronouncement 'only connect', by his fellow Apostle E. M. Forster, was. Keynes was fairly plain about this when he later declared that although he and his circle had accepted the final chapter, they had disregarded the penultimate one dealing with Moore's views on Ethics as they relate to conduct. As Keynes put it 'we recognised no moral obligation on us, no inner sanction, to conform or to obey' and, at another point, 'we accepted Moore's religion, so to speak, and discarded his morals'. Leonard Woolf, in marked contrast, flatly denied Keynes's statement that they had neglected all that Moore said about morals and rules of conduct. What we see in this contradiction is not so much a difference in understanding as a difference in temperament. And this split between the moralists and the amoralists (or immoralists) was carried over into Bloomsbury intact. Being a disciple of Moore meant very different things to the different people who became part of Bloomsbury.

The second peculiarity of the Society in relation to its membership was that during each generation some individual more or less dominated the Society, largely controlling its proceedings and, in particular, its admission of new members. The leadership of F. D. Maurice in the mid-nineteenth century was succeeded by that of Henry Sidgwick, followed by Ellis McTaggart who, in turn, was succeeded by G. E. Moore — each, it so happens, a teacher of moral philosophy at Trinity College. This leadership position was informal and subtle, hence there seems to have been no dramatic crisis — possibly the event was not even noticed at the time — when two relatively new members of the Society, Lytton Strachey and Maynard Keynes, both aggressive and quite sure of themselves, and neither of them moral philosophers, became the dominant voices. Perhaps one of the reasons the event may not have been noticed is that Strachey and Keynes were disciples of Moore and he, still a young man, continued to take an active part in the affairs of the Society.

* In the Preface to *Principia Ethica* Moore says that his 'main object' was to establish 'the fundamental principles of ethical reasoning ... rather than of any conclusions which may be attained by their use' (ix).

Strachey, 'going through the Society's papers in his role as secretary ... had become convinced that many past Apostles were in fact secret and non-practising homosexuals'. He and Keynes, operating under no such constraints, began putting far more emphasis on the personal attractiveness of the embryos: 'he looks pink and delightful as embryos should' wrote Strachey of a new prospect. Strachey and Keynes worked hard for their candidates. In order to gain admission into the Society for this 'pink and delightful' prospect they managed to overcome the tradition against the selection of men in their first year and then, once the objective had been gained, Strachey and Keynes fought between themselves for his affection. Bertrand Russell states in his autobiography that, since Lytton Strachey's time, 'homosexual relations among the members were for a time common, but in my day they were unknown'.

This represented another division among the seven Apostles who were to become the founding fathers of Bloomsbury: Strachey and Keynes were practising homosexuals; E. M. Forster, always latently so disposed, and considerably older than Strachey and Keynes, seems to have become an active homosexual after the two younger men had made their propensities known. Leonard Woolf, Roger Fry and Desmond McCarthy were heterosexual. Saxon Sydney-Turner here, as everywhere, remains an enigma. 'Saxon can't decide anything', wrote Virginia to Vanessa in 1909, 'even what he wants to eat.'

The third element in the impact of the Society on its members was its pervasiveness. Association between members was not limited to the weekly meeting in Cambridge and the annual meeting in London. Although each of the Apostles had other friends and associates, the strongest ties were with fellow members: 'We not only called ourselves, but felt and acted like brothers,' wrote Walter Leaf. This included meeting daily and nightly throughout term time; taking reading holidays together and visiting each other's homes during vacations. They corresponded with each other; they confided in each other; they looked to fellow Apostles for advice. And in many instances this continued throughout their lifetimes. The statement by Henry Sidgwick that 'the tie of attachment to the society is much the strongest corporate bond which I have known in life' was the prevailing view among many if not most Apostles. Thus it is not at all surprising that at some point a convenient place of congregating outside Cambridge should have been found for some of the Apostles who had gone down from the university.

[3]

THE APOSTLES IN
BLOOMSBURY

37 *Lytton Strachey in 1917 at Lord's Wood, Alix Sargant-Florence's house
near Marlow*

The nineteenth-century aphorism that 'When German philosophers die
they go to Oxford' had its Cambridge counterpart in the twentieth
century: when the Apostles took wing they went to Bloomsbury.

Since the definition of Bloomsbury continues to be a source of conten-
tion and misunderstanding it should be remembered that there are at
least three Bloomsburies. First, of course, there is the geographical area
which, like Greenwich Village in New York or the Latin Quarter in
Paris, has no legally defined boundaries, but is thought of as south of

Euston Road, west of Gray's Inn Road, north of New Oxford Street and Holborn and east of Tottenham Court Road—the area that took its name from the Blemond family whose manor or *burh* stood there in the thirteenth century. Second, there is the general mass of intellectuals and bohemians that moved into the once quiet residential area when it began to become a bit shabby in the second half of the nineteenth century. The proximity of the British Museum (the great domed reading room was opened in 1858), the easy access to Fleet Street, and the low rents brought a stream of students, writers and artists that has never ended. Swinburne lived in Guilford Street until 1879; Havelock Ellis, in 1894, established a Fellowship of the New Life commune espousing free love at 29 Doughty Street. A flippant playwright, in 1902, made one of his characters say 'the Bloomsburians live mainly on a dish called "smoked 'addick"'.

Then, a few years later, the Apostles came to Bloomsbury. Not all the Apostles but enough of the younger ones, with a few outsiders, to create a little metropolitan adjunct to the Cambridge Society. This select group, an informal one, gradually acquired the name of 'Bloomsbury', and the resulting confusion between this particular group and the rest of humanity living in the area has not been resolved by the fact that its members have spent a great deal of time arguing that there was no such group, and an equal amount of time arguing about who belonged to it.

To create a graduate Apostolic establishment in London it was necessary that there be a meeting place; not simply any meeting place but one—like student accommodations at the University—where neither the hours of coming and going nor the conduct of the occupants would be impeded by the susceptibilities of parents or other elderly relatives. By what must be regarded as sheer chance, a meeting place satisfying these requirements was provided late in 1904 by the four children of Leslie Stephen.

Leslie Stephen had died of abdominal cancer in February 1904 after an illness that had lasted nearly two years. During this extended interval Virginia had borne most of the emotional burden. Vanessa had long been out of sympathy with her father because of the demands he made on her as head of the household, and those he made on both of his daughters for affection. Virginia had always had a strong attachment to her father, and although she resented his demands, she could appreciate his integrity, his underlying humility and his intelligence. Almost daily reports of his illness were sent to a new friend, Violet Dickinson, a woman seventeen years older than Virginia—'very slapdash and jocular'—to whom Virginia looked for moral support at a time when Vanessa was unable to share her feelings about their father. When Leslie Stephen died Virginia had worrying dreams of him and was wrung by a feeling of guilt: she felt that she could have done so much more for him while he was living. To distract her, she was taken off by her brothers and sister first to Wales, and then to Italy and France. But by the time they returned, in May 1904, it was apparent that Virginia was suffering from a second mental breakdown. She expressed complete distrust of Vanessa, possibly because of Vanessa's attitude toward their father, and was removed to Violet Dickinson's house in Hertfordshire. There she heard 'voices', birds singing in Greek, Edward VII uttering obscenities in the garden — and made a suicide attempt by jumping out of a window too close to the ground to do any damage to herself. After three months at Burnham Wood and another three months with members of her family, Virginia was able to go home: to a new home in Bloomsbury. For within seven months of Leslie Stephen's death the practical Vanessa had cleaned out the debris of three generations of Stephens from 22 Hyde Park Gate, and moved brothers and sisters to 46 Gordon Square. Virginia's explanation of the move was that 'Vanessa looking at a map of London and seeing how far apart they were — had decided that we should leave Kensington and start life afresh in Bloomsbury.'

Bloomsbury was not a good address: 'When our old family friends and relations made the difficult journey to Bloomsbury ... they threw up their heads and snuffed the air. They explored the house suspiciously', wrote Virginia. 'I can still see the vast bulk of cousin Mia Macnamara looming in the hall and expressing by the tilt of her bonnet, the heaving of her tremendous bosom, and the glare of her small beady eyes her apprehension and disapproval ... There was something in the atmosphere; something hostile to the old traditions of the family; something she knew my mother would have disapproved of for her daughters.' But notwithstanding the attitude of elderly relatives, 46 Gordon Square provided what was wanted. It was light and cheerful. Both Virginia and Vanessa had a sitting-room; there was a large double dining-room and a study on the ground floor. Although the contingency was surely not in the mind of Vanessa when she found the place, there was plenty of meeting space for the Apostles and their friends, and none of the constraints of a typical Victorian household.

Neither Thoby nor Adrian were members of the Society, but several of Thoby's friends were. Vanessa and Virginia had met these friends at Cambridge and for years had listened to Thoby's romantic accounts of them. There was Lytton Strachey: 'the Strache', Thoby called him. As related by Virginia: 'The Strache was the essence of culture. In fact I think his culture a little alarmed Thoby. He had French pictures in his rooms. He had a passion for Pope. He was exotic, extreme in every way. Thoby described him—so long, so thin that his thigh was no thicker than Thoby's arm. Once he went into Thoby's rooms, cried out, "Do you hear the music of the spheres?" and fell in a faint. Once in the midst of a dead silence he piped up—and Thoby could imitate his voice perfectly—"Let's all write sonnets to Robertson". He was a prodigy of wit. Even the tutors and the dons would come and listen to him. "Whatever they give you, Strachey", Dr. Jackson had said when Strachey was in for some examination, "it won't be good enough".'

And there was Saxon Sydney-Turner. 'According to Thoby, Sydney-Turner ... had the whole of Greek literature by heart. There was practically nothing in any language that was any good that he had not read. He was very silent and thin and odd. He never came out by day. But late at night if he saw one's lamp burning he would come and tap at the window like a moth. At about three in the morning he would begin to talk. His talk was then of astonishing brilliance'. Virginia added, 'When later I complained to Thoby that I had not found Turner brilliant Thoby severely supposed that by brilliance I meant wit; he on the contrary meant truth.'

On Thursday evening, March 2, 1905, several months after the Stephens had moved to Gordon Square, Strachey and Sydney-Turner 'came after dinner and we talked till twelve'. Three weeks later, on a Thursday evening, a total of nine 'came to our evening and stayed till one'. There were a few non-Apostles among the callers: Clive Bell, for example. Through his association with the Apostles he was indoctrinated with much of their philosophy. Not unnaturally, Bell also was an avowed disciple of G. E. Moore. Within a week of the initial appearance of Strachey and Sydney-Turner at Gordon Square, Bell turned up, and according to Virginia on his first visit 'we talked ... about the nature of Good till one'.

Bell had also been described by Thoby to Virginia: 'There's an astonishing fellow called Bell ... he's a sort of mixture between Shelley and a sporting country squire ... We were walking over a moor somewhere I remember. I got a fantastic impression that this man Bell was a kind of sun God—with straw in his hair ... Bell had never opened a book till he came to Cambridge, Thoby said. Then he suddenly discovered Shelley and Keats and went nearly mad with excitement. He did nothing but spout poetry and write poetry. Yet he was a perfect horseman—a gift which Thoby enormously admired—and kept two or three hunters up at Cambridge.'

Leonard Woolf, although a visitor at 46 Gordon Square in November 1904, a month after the Stephens moved in, almost immediately left for Ceylon, where he stayed for seven years, and therefore did not participate in any of the first Thursday evening gatherings out of which 'Bloomsbury' grew. The regulars at these gatherings included not only those mentioned: Strachey, Sydney-Turner and Bell, but their friends — mostly Cambridge, mostly disciples of Moore, mostly Apostles. Among the others as time went on were R. G. Hawtrey, Desmond MacCarthy, Robin Mayor, Theodore Llewelyn Davies, C. P. Sanger, H. J. T. Norton, James Strachey, Maynard Keynes, J. T. Sheppard, Duncan Grant, Walter Headlam, Sydney Waterlow, Walter Lamb, Hilton Young, Jack Pollock — all Cambridge except Duncan Grant (a first cousin of Lytton Strachey), and all Apostles except the last six. They brought with them Moore's clarity, his taciturnity and his ethics. Listening to these young men and matching wits with them provided Virginia with many of the fundamentals of the university education which she lacked, and drove her to read what they had read so she could hold her own:

> From such discussions Vanessa and I got probably much the same pleasure that undergraduates get when they meet friends of their own for the first time. At last we could use our brains. And part of the charm of those Thursday evenings was that they were astonishingly abstract. It was not only that Moore's book had set us all discussing philosophy, art, religion; it was that the atmosphere ... was abstract in the extreme. The young men ... criticised our arguments as severely as their own ... In that world the only comment we allowed ourselves after our guests had gone was 'I must say you made your point rather well' or 'I think you were talking rather through your hat'.

This life — four Stephens at 46 Gordon Square with their Thursday evening gatherings — continued for over two years, a period which Virginia, in a paper read to the Memoir Club sometime in the 1920s, called 'Chapter One' of the history of Bloomsbury. In Chapter One, Virginia was thoroughly indoctrinated in the precision of thought and expression demanded by the author of *Principia Ethica* and was schooled in his conclusions on the nature of Good. It was also during this period that she began to move into a world outside the homes of relatives and friends. In November 1904, nine months after her father's death, she sent some articles to *The Guardian*, a weekly periodical published in London, and in its columns appeared in print for the first time. In the following year she began writing for *The Times Literary Supplement*, and also started to teach classes for the working people who attended Morley College. Although she remained friendly with Violet Dickinson, she also received sympathy and understanding from Madge Vaughan, a woman thirteen years older than herself who had married one of Virginia's cousins.

At 46 Gordon Square the Stephen family was able to regain some of the cheerfulness of St Ives; they revisited Cornwall together in 1905 and peered through the hedge at Talland House, where they had spent so many joyous childhood days. In the following year all four — Vanessa, Thoby, Virginia and Adrian — went off to Greece accompanied by Violet Dickinson. But these happy days proved even more transient than those of earlier times, for during the trip Thoby contracted typhoid fever and after a month's illness died on November 20. Two days later, almost as a reflex, Vanessa agreed to marry Thoby's friend Clive Bell, who had been pursuing her for some time.

In 'Chapter Two' Vanessa and Clive continued to live at 46 Gordon Square after their marriage, while Virginia and Adrian moved to a house in nearby Fitzroy Square, a house they shared for four years (1907–11). Virginia's emotional ties had always been with Thoby and Vanessa and once again she was lonely. Mother, father, brother and now sister, she felt, were gone. In her struggle to recapture what was lost Virginia was repeatedly drawn back to Cornwall, symbol of the intact family of earlier days. She returned six times in the period 1908–10, once by herself — alone — to celebrate Christmas, the day most likely to recall family gatherings. Life with Adrian at Fitzroy Square was distinctly not a success. 'We were the most incompatible of people', wrote Virginia. 'We drove each other perpetually into frenzies of irritation or into the depths of gloom.' Even the Thursday night meetings palled. 'We ... still had Thursday evenings as before. But they were always strained and often ended in dismal failure. Adrian stalked off to his room, I to mine, in complete silence.'

The strain of the Thursday evenings was not, however, entirely or even mainly due to the incompatibility of Virginia and Adrian, or to the existence of a second salon in Gordon Square. The visitors seemed to have run out of subjects to discuss. This, it shortly appeared, was because they had not, up to then, followed the essential precept of the Apostles in Cambridge that 'there were to be no *taboos*, no limitations, nothing considered shocking'. They had skirted their interpretation of the statement in *Principia Ethica* that 'the love of love, is far the most valuable good we know, and far more valuable than the love of beauty'. In brief, Sex — whether heterosexual or homosexual — had been a taboo topic, and it was the single topic in which most of the young men attending the meetings were most interested. Harkening back to the days of her 'Chapter One', Virginia recalled:

I knew that there were buggers in Plato's Greece; I suspected—it was not a question one could ask Thoby—that there were buggers in Dr. Butler's Trinity, but it never occurred to me that there were buggers even now in the Stephen sitting room at Gordon Square. It never struck me that the abstractness, the simplicity which had been so great a relief after Hyde Park Gate were largely due to the fact that the majority of young men who came there were not attracted by young women.

A year or so after the death of Thoby and the marriage of Vanessa, the taboo was shattered. The final barrier to completely free discussion was removed, and Sex, which loomed so large in the lives of most of the young Apostles of the day, became the principal topic of conversation.

Sex permeated our conversation. The word bugger was never far from our lips. We discussed copulation with the same excitement and openness that we had discussed the nature of good. It is strange to think how reticent, how reserved we had been and for how long ... Now we talked of nothing else ... we listened with rapt interest to the love affairs of the buggers. We followed the ups and downs of their chequered histories, Vanessa sympathetically; I—it is one of the differences between us—frivolously, laughingly.

This description, written by Virginia years after the event, suggests that she was never fully sympathetic to the buggers. Indeed, in one of her letters to Lytton in 1912 she states that the 'ap-s-les' (mocking their secrecy) and their 'unreal' loves made her vomit. The rational Virginia with Apostolic indoctrination, for whom there were no constraints, must always be distinguished from the emotional Virginia with a deeply rooted puritanism derived from her ancestry. Even when she was 58 years old she held to the view that 'nothing in the whole world is so lyrical, so musical, as a young man and a young woman in their first love for each other'—and she went on to emphasise that she was referring to 'respectable engagements' and not 'unofficial love'.

Since she was able to retain this romantic view of 'respectable' love throughout a life that had witnessed, as a bystander, every type of deviation from Victorian standards, it is all the more remarkable that she was able to talk calmly of buggery and copulation in her rooms at 29 Fitzroy Square in the first decade of the twentieth century. But talk she did.* Thus by the end of Chapter Two, which came in 1911, Bloomsbury had become a full-fledged offshoot of the Apostles, devoid of all taboos, but with one important difference: it was no longer an all-male society. Virginia and Vanessa were at the centre of it.

---

* Yet in 1924 she wrote: 'sexual relations bore me more than they used: am I a prude?'

38 *Leonard with the Ratemahatmayas outside the Kandy kachcheri*

39 *Leonard with a hunting party*

[4]

AN APOSTLE
IN THE JUNGLE

40 *Leonard with his horse Blackbird*

One of the papers read by Leonard as an undergraduate member of the Society was called 'George or George or Both?' It posed the question whether the proper Apostolic life was that of contemplation, à la Apostle George Moore, or that of action, à la Apostle George Trevelyan, or some combination of the two. The paper straddled the issue, coming to the conclusion that the contemplative George (Moore) should become active to the extent of writing a new Education Act for Britain.

This compromise to some extent foreshadowed Leonard's own career, which was shaped, as so many careers have been, by chance as much as by choice. When he went up to Cambridge in 1899 he had a vague intention of becoming a barrister, having as a small boy announced that he would be 'what Papa was and drive every morning in a brougham to King's Bench Walk'. For reasons we do not know, this intention was altered not once but several times over the next few years. In his third year in the Classical Tripos, Part I, Leonard got a First Class, but only in the third division, a sharp disappointment to him and to Dr Butler, Master of Trinity. Leonard stayed up for a fourth year, reading for Part II of the Classical Tripos, which covered Greek philosophy—presumably in the hope that he might get a Fellowship. This effort proved even more disappointing, for he got only a Second Class. Then he stayed on another year, reading for the Civil Service examination, in which he did very badly indeed, standing 69th among those taking the examination that year. None of these tests had Leonard taken sufficiently seriously; having the highest confidence in his own intelligence, he neglected to refresh his familiarity with certain syllabus classics or to be tutored in the subjects traditionally covered in the Civil Service examinations. His exceptionally low standing meant that he could not expect appointment in the choice services: the Treasury or the Foreign Office. As he explained in *Sowing*:

The best that I could hope for was a place in the Post Office or Inland Revenue. I was over age for India. I felt that I could not face a lifetime to be spent in Somerset House or in the Post Office, so I decided to take an appointment in the Colonial Service, then called Eastern Cadetships. I applied for Ceylon, which was the senior Crown Colony, and was high enough up on the list to get what I asked for. I found myself to my astonishment and, it must be admitted, dismay in the Ceylon Civil Service.

'Astonishment' and 'dismay' represent recollection in tranquillity fifty years after the event. At the time, the situation seemed far more desperate. Leonard wrote to G. E. Moore on October 4, 1904: 'I am in a horrible state of mind and complete despair. I have taken an Eastern cadetship … I do hate the thought of it all, but I was simply overwhelmed by circumstances.'

This resignation to a life in the Colonial Service, this dismissal of the other alternatives still available to him (including his first love, the bar), was perhaps partly due to pique, but was more probably dictated by lack of money. Reading for the bar, then as now, involved supporting yourself for several years before there was any prospect of becoming independent, and Leonard had no private means whatever. Once having decided upon this new course he made no effort to extricate himself; instead, he spent the latter part of 1904 preparing for departure. He bought tropical gear. He learned to ride in Knightsbridge Barracks. He passed his medical examination with the equivocal compliment of having the cleanest feet of anyone the doctor had examined that morning. He said goodbye to his family, his Apostolic 'brothers', friends, and to the Stephens of 46 Gordon Square. And in November 1904* he set sail for Colombo on the P & O S.S. *Syria*.

In the second volume of his autobiography Leonard describes his six-and-a-half years in Ceylon. The story is unfolded chronologically: Jaffna from 1905 to 1907; Kandy from 1907 to 1908; Hambantota from 1908 to 1911. In one sense it is an account of Leonard's official duties and of his social life during these years. In a larger sense it is an account of how an 'embittered and disappointed youth'—an 'arrogant, conceited and quick tempered young man'—to use his own words, hardened his heart 'against the past and against regret for the past'; how, in short, he earned the right to re-enter the Apostolic life on which he had turned his back.

An essential part of this process of purgation was the attainment of a satisfactory level of success in the new career. At five different points in his account of life in Ceylon, Leonard assures himself and his readers that he had been 'extremely' or 'extraordinarily' or 'highly' competent in the performance of his duties. And so he was. In an atmosphere more conducive to relaxation than exertion, he put in ten or eleven hours a day at his work. He learned to write, read and speak Tamil and then Sinhalese. He studied law so that he could function as a magistrate. He constantly sought increased responsibility. He rode all day in the tropical sun. He struggled from his sickbed back to the job. 'I work, God, how I work. I have reduced it to a method and exalted it to a mania.'

At the outset Leonard was occupied principally with paper work; issuing permits, answering inquiries and preparing reports for his superiors at the Jaffna *kachcheri*, the local government headquarters. After he had been at Jaffna for a year he created a paper-work revolution:

Whenever I came new into an office in Ceylon, I would find 10, 20 or 30 great files waiting on my table to be dealt with and only 5 to 10 per cent of the ordinary routine letters would be answered on the day they were received ... On my second day in the office I always sent for the head clerk and said to him: 'Every letter received in this *kachcheri* after this week must be answered on the

---

* Not October 1904 as stated in the autobiography.

day of its receipt unless it is waiting for an order from me or from the G.A.' The answer of the head clerk was always that in this office the number of letters received daily is so large that it would be totally impossible to answer them in the same day. And the answer to that was: 'You are receiving in this office 500 letters a day, or 13,000 a month. Nine out of the ten letters which you answer today were received in the office five or six days ago. But the number of unanswered letters at the beginning of the month is on the average the same as the number of unanswered letters at the end of the month. So you are in fact answering about 500 letters every day ... Therefore if you once catch up—as I insist upon your doing—you will find that you will save yourself and everyone else an immense amount of time and worry.'

*　　*　　*

I told the head clerk that he should let everyone know that I proposed to inspect the whole *kachcheri* and every clerk's desk ... until I found that the Record Department was up to date and every letter was being as a general rule answered on the day of its receipt. All this made me extremely unpopular and I got the reputation ... of being a strict and ruthless civil servant ... But as time went by they completely changed their view of my methods of business organisation, and nearly all of them agreed that my revolution had not only enormously increased efficiency but made their own work easier.

Leonard demonstrated his efficiency in other less conventional ways in his second assignment at Kandy, on one occasion arranging a private viewing of Buddha's tooth for Empress Eugénie and on another providing a spectacular show of native dancing for the Acting Governor and his party, including a lady whom the Acting Governor was anxious to impress. Then, after three-and-a-half years of service, Leonard was made Assistant Government Agent at Hambantota, directly responsible for 100,000 people living in an area of 1,000 square miles. 'This was extraordinarily rapid promotion', Leonard explains, 'for I was the youngest A.G.A. and three years younger than the next youngest A.G.A.'

The new appointment making Woolf, in Strachey's imagination, 'Lord of a million blacks', was a stimulus to renewed effort:

In the $2\frac{3}{4}$ years in Hambantota, it is almost true to say, I worked all day from the moment I got up in the morning until the moment I went to bed at night, for I rarely thought of anything else except the District and the people, to increase their prosperity, diminish the poverty and disease, start irrigation works, open schools.

Leonard offers two examples to prove this: first, despite the topographical difficulties encountered in Hambantota, his district was the first to complete the census taken in 1911, a distinction which was the subject of considerable rivalry among the various A.G.A's. Second, utilising new methods of Leonard's own making, the Hambantota Dis-

41-2 *Leonard took with him to Ceylon a dog named Charles that he had at Cambridge. When the climate proved too much for Charles he was replaced by a succession of other dogs*

43

44

5

6

43-5 *Three native scenes in Ceylon*

46 *The pearl fishery at Marichchukaddi*

47 *The court at Kandy*

trict collected more salt than at any other time in the history of the station. His other successes, although not capable of equivalent quantitative measurement, were none the less distinctive. For a period of nearly two years he fought the Rinderpest, a dreaded and disgusting destroyer of cattle and buffaloes. After the battle against this disease had been won, at the cost of a huge loss in animals, Leonard introduced modern ploughs (he taught himself to use the equipment in order to do this) to take the place of the buffaloes previously used to 'muddle' the fields—the traditional method of preparing the paddies for sowing by driving the animals round and round until the soil has been stirred up. (As soon as Leonard left the district the farmers returned to muddling.)

In another effort to modernise methods, Leonard induced a syndicate of landowners to buy a simple threshing machine costing £15:

A large crowd came to see it and it was most successful. It threshes very cleanly and requires actually to work it only two men ... The only drawback is that the people persist in working machines with all nuts and bolts loose so they are bound to break and another is that they are so careless that I am sure someone will get his hand threshed as well as the paddy.

Leonard's efforts were not limited to collecting facts and minerals or to combating diseases and introducing machines. He had important responsibilities for people. On one occasion he superintended the great Kataragama Pilgrimage—one Englishman, 29 years old, with no staff or police force, responsible for the order and well-being of nearly 4,000 people in the heart of the jungle. On several occasions he worked out compromises in seemingly unresolvable controversies between landowners and rival religious groups. Leonard wrote his own epitaph on his final civil service duties: 'I set out to make the Hambantota District the best administered in the island, and I do not think that I deceive or flatter myself when I say that I succeeded.'

As can be seen, the process of hardening his heart against the past and against regret for the past was not through outward humility. Leonard was determined, from the start, to stand out as a distinctive personality both in his official life and in his social life in Ceylon. His appearance at Jaffna in January 1905 made it clear that here was no ordinary phenomenon. He brought with him to this remote outpost of the Empire a wooden case containing the complete works of Voltaire in 70 volumes.* His wardrobe included green flannel collars of a type that had never been seen in Ceylon. Another of his self-denominated 'assets' was a dog that quickly established its ability to kill local cats and snakes in a business-

---

* Not 90 volumes as repeatedly stated in the autobiography.

like manner. In his first game of bridge in Jaffna the newly arrived cadet struck a blow for social freedom by calling a revoke on the local bridge tyrant, and then proving his allegation.

This man-of-the-world carapace was carefully cultivated by Leonard. He bought whisky six cases at a time. He was visited by the local whores. He took part in all the sports that were going: tennis, golf, swimming, squash, cricket, hockey, polo. He saved a man from drowning. He owned a horse and kept three or four dogs. He joined the Ceylon Mounted Rifles. He shot game and in the single year 1910 recorded a total bag of 45 snipe, 15 teal, 19 green pigeons, 2 imperial pigeons, 2 jungle cock, 4 jungle fowl, 7 golden plover, 5 hare and 9 deer. He played cards for money and made bets on practically everything from American politics to local romances. He won £17 in one sweepstake and £690 in another, and his less fortunate (and possibly less thrifty) associates frequently borrowed money from him. His reputation carried on after he left Ceylon, for it was even rumoured there that he had inherited £60,000 on the sinking of the *Titanic* in 1912.

Scrupulously fair, but (as he himself admits in his autobiography) outwardly truculent and often ruthless to the natives to save them from themselves, Leonard enjoyed his spiritual flagellation in private. Leonard's letters to Lytton Strachey, his Apostolic confidant and closest friend, were filled with gloom about his dull, incompetent and pompous associates; the sordidness of many of the natives; the decay and drudgery of the *kachcheris*; the uncomfortable climate; the fevers, the eczema, the ringworm, the headaches and the diarrhoea. Writing to Strachey in 1905 he referred to himself as a 'mediocrity' and a 'failure'—meaning in Strachey's world, since he added, 'Here, of course, I am considered anything but a failure.' He discussed the possibility of suicide in March 1906 and a month later wrote 'I took out my gun the other night, made my will and prepared to shoot myself.' In 1907 he asserted 'I'm done for as regards England. I shall live and die in these appalling countries now.'

Work and despair were two of the recurring themes in these letters to Strachey. The other two were the Apostles and women. The Society and its members were discussed in nearly every letter; Apostolic standards were applied to all aspects of life in Ceylon; Leonard's copy of *Principia Ethica* was lent to whomever would read it. G. E. Moore, called the 'Yen' by his young admirers, remained Leonard's idol: 'I should like beyond all things to be the Yen.' Moore's attitude toward marriage made a deep impression on him: ' ... one of the saddest things in Moore's letter I thought was this. He said that Ainsworth seemed so happy at being engaged. "I wished I could be engaged too!" '

From the outset of Leonard's stay, women had been a source of disquiet. 'Women seem to me absolutely the abomination of desolation, in Ceylon at any rate.' A month after writing this he reported that he was in love with his superior's wife, a woman substantially older than he was but 'the only person—male or female—in Jaffna not positively repulsive to look at'. Then he enjoyed a carefully controlled flirtation with another older woman, a rather ugly spinster who had pathetically and hopelessly fallen in love with him. Next came the 18-year-old girl called 'Gwen' in Leonard's autobiography: 'After the fierce heat of the day a gentle, languid, and pleasant melancholy would settle over the lagoon and over us as we lay on the seaweedy sand platonically—if that is the right word —in each other's arms. For many years ... whenever I suddenly get the strong smell of seaweed, as in the town of Worthing, I get a vivid vision of Gwen and the sands of Jaffna.' Gwen must have had her visions too, since for the next fifty years she kept Leonard's dog 'Argus' (stuffed, of course) on a shelf in her room. Then there was Rachel Robinson with whom Leonard galloped in the woods above Kandy and 'reached the maximum of intimacy ... allowed by the extraordinary etiquette and reticencies of the age'.

Leonard conscientiously reported each episode to Strachey, at one point observing 'I am beginning to think it is always degraded being in love: after all 99/100ths of it is always the desire to copulate, otherwise it is only the shadow of itself, and a particular desire to copulate seems to me no less degraded than a general'. Leonard, who thought perhaps he was 'only in love with silly intrigue and controlling a situation', managed to control things reasonably well by Victorian standards, seeking his satisfaction from the readily available prostitutes of Jaffna—but apparently small satisfaction it was since, as he reported to Strachey, he found horse riding in the jungle 'better I think as a pleasure than copulation'.

It is plain that what Leonard found 'degrading' in his romances was the object of his affections. By both persuasion and nature Leonard was a G. E. Moore man to the core, and 'wherever the affection is most valuable' says *Principia Ethica*, 'the appreciation of mental qualities must form a large part of it'. Leonard admired Gwen's body, but he could see right through her 'two big cow eyes which could never understand anything which one said' even though they looked 'as if they understood everything that has ever been, is or will be'.

One difficulty, perhaps, was that Leonard had known women who *could* understand what one said, and this image was kept constantly before him during the years of Ceylon servitude. When Clive Bell— the bumptious, fox-hunting, non-apostolic Bell—had the audacity to propose to Vanessa Stephen in the summer of 1905, this alarming news was promptly relayed to Leonard, who replied:

Your letter was chiefly about Bell. It's rather sad, certainly more so than I thought it was for I always saw that he was in love with one of them—though strangely I thought it was the other. In a way I should like never to come back again now ... You think that Bell is really wildly in love with her? The curious part is that I was too after they came up that May term to Cambridge and still more curious that there is a mirage of it still left. She is so superbly like the Goth.* I often used to wonder whether he was in love with the Goth because he was in love with her and I was in love with her, because with the Goth. At any rate I give it to you as a palliation.

The suggestion that Leonard's first interest was Vanessa, rather than Virginia, coincides with the statement in his autobiography that he thought Vanessa 'usually more beautiful than Virginia. The form of her features was more perfect, her eyes bigger and better, her complexion more glowing.'

Clive Bell was not accepted by Vanessa in 1905. He was accepted a year and a half later, immediately following the death of her brother Thoby. They were married in February 1907. But even after the marriage Clive continued his flirtation with Virginia. In 1908, Clive, Vanessa and Virginia went to Italy together—an event also duly reported by Strachey to Leonard in Ceylon:

Clive has been to Italy for September with those sisters. Don't you think it's the wildest romance? That that little canary-coloured creature we knew in the New Court should have achieved that? The two most beautiful and wittiest women in England! He's certainly lucky.

A month later, possibly stimulated by Clive's success, Lytton wrote to Leonard saying 'don't be surprised whatever may happen, or if you hear one day—I don't know that you ever will—that I've married Virginia.' After this astounding declaration, Lytton must have expressed some doubts in correspondence that has been lost. For the next letter we have is one from Leonard to Lytton early in 1909:

But I don't agree with you. The most wonderful of all would have been to marry Virginia. She is I imagine supreme and then the final solution would have been there, not a rise perhaps above all horrors but certainly not a fall, not a shirking of facts ... but it certainly would be the only thing. It is undoubtedly the only way to happiness.

Then, shifting to his own unmarried state, Leonard remarks: 'something

* Thoby Stephen.

or other always saves me just at the last moment from these degradations —their lasciviousness or their ugliness probably—though I believe if I did I should probably be happy. Do you think Virginia would have me? Wire to me if she accepts. I'll take the next boat home.' As a final twist, Leonard ends his letter, 'I wonder if after all Virginia marries Turner'.

This letter was received by Lytton on February 19, 1909. Two days earlier Lytton had, temporarily at least, resolved his doubts about marrying Virginia and had proposed to her. On receipt of Leonard's letter he replied:

Your letter has this minute come—with your proposal to Virginia ... The day before yesterday I proposed to Virginia. As I did it, I saw that it would be death if she accepted me, and I managed, of course, to get out of it before the end of the conversation. The worst of it was that as the conversation went on, it became more and more obvious to me that the whole thing was impossible. The lack of understanding was so terrific! And how can a virgin be expected to understand? You see she *is* her name ... It was, as you may imagine, an amazing conversation. Her sense was absolute, and at times her supremacy was so great that I quavered. I think there's no doubt whatever that you ought to marry her. You *would* be great enough, and you'd have too the immense advantage of physical desire. I was in terror lest she should kiss me. If you came and proposed she'd accept. She really really would. As it is, she's almost certainly in love with me, though she thinks she's not.

A final paragraph added the next day reads:

I've had an eclaircissement with Virginia.
She declared she was not in love with me, and I observed finally that I would not marry her. So things have simply reverted. Perhaps you'd better not mention these matters to Turner, who certainly is not upon the tapis. I told Vanessa to hand on your proposal, so perhaps *you* are.

Whether Vanessa ever did 'hand on' Leonard's proposal to Virginia we do not know. If she did, the long-distance wooing by proxy must have provided a good deal of merriment to the two sisters. But perhaps it did serve its purpose on Virginia's side by adding another candidate to her growing list of suitors, which at this point or shortly thereafter included Saxon Sydney-Turner, Walter Lamb, Hilton Young, Sydney Waterlow and Harry Norton.* On Leonard's side, the encouragement given by Lytton opened up a prospect which may have previously seemed unattainable to him. Although this encouragement at first possibly sounded perfunctory, Lytton had not intended that it should be—following up with two other letters on the same theme. On May 27, 1909 he wrote to Leonard:

* Walter Headlam had died in 1908.

Perhaps you're packing up to come home—that would be the most satisfactory thing. If you come, as I think I've mentioned, you could marry Virginia, which should settle nearly every difficulty in the best possible way. Do try it. She's an astounding woman, and I'm the only man in the universe who could have refused her; even I sometimes have my doubts. You might, of course, propose by telegram, and she'd probably accept. That would be very fine; but in any case you'll have to come back.

Two months later, on August 21, 1909, Lytton resumed the subject with increasing urgency:

Your destiny is clearly marked out for you, but will you allow it to work? You must marry Virginia. She's sitting waiting for you, is there any objection? She's the only woman in the world with sufficient brains; its a miracle that she should exist; but if you're not careful you'll lose the opportunity. At any moment she might go off with heaven knows who—Duncan? Quite possible. She's young, wild, inquisitive, discontented, and longing to be in love. If I were you I should telegraph. But at any rate come and see her before the end of 1910 ... Saxon (as he's now called) is I believe at this moment in Bayreuth with Virginia and Adrian. But you're safe so far as *he's* concerned; only I don't know what charming German Barons may not be there. Telegraph.

What happened after this letter we do not know. Although Leonard and Lytton had exchanged approximately 200 letters in the period November 1904 to August 1909, not a single letter on either side is known to exist for the period August 1909 to January 1911. Knowing the individuals, we can make a fair guess that Lytton would have kept Leonard's name before Virginia, that Virginia was laughingly evasive and that Leonard, in his hermitage at Hambantota, brooded on the lovely vision he had first seen in Cambridge 'that May term', but without much hope of realisation. And as time went on, he must have had increasing doubts as to whether his destiny was 'clearly marked out for him' as Strachey had predicted in 1909.

On May 24, 1911, after six-and-a-half years in Ceylon, Leonard sailed from Colombo for England—presumably for a 12-month spell of leave. He left the 70 volumes of Voltaire, his horse, his dogs and guns and his other possessions behind him. He was 31 years old and had made a good start on a career in the Ceylon Civil Service.

[5]

COURTSHIP
AND MARRIAGE

48 *Leonard and Virginia on their wedding day*

When Leonard arrived in England on June 11, 1911 he went directly to his mother's home in Putney. Even after this duty had been performed, he did not rush to throw himself at Virginia; instead, he did precisely what he had said he would do two years before when he told Strachey that if there was a chance that Virginia would have him he would 'come straight to talk to you'. Thus, on June 14, Leonard went to talk to Strachey, who was living in Cambridge. What passed between Leonard and Lytton we do not know. But a good guess would be that Leonard learned about Virginia's principal suitors (at the moment Walter Lamb was the most active) and was advised to see Vanessa, Lytton's confidant in his pursuit of Virginia. So Leonard saw Vanessa. On July 3 he had dinner with Vanessa and Clive Bell at their house in Gordon Square. After dinner, according to Leonard's diary, 'Duncan Grant, Virginia and Walter Lamb came in'.

Five days later Virginia, in a letter addressed to 'Mr. Wolf', invited Leonard to spend a weekend at the small place she had rented at Firle, in Sussex. Because of conflicting engagements this did not take place until the weekend of September 16–19, when Marjorie Strachey was coming. Until this meeting, despite the plans their friends had been making for them, Virginia and Leonard had little first-hand knowledge of each other. It is doubtful whether they had ever been alone together before.* Now they talked and walked on the Downs. 'Walked Alfriston tea, back about 9. Talked w. V until 1' is Leonard's diary entry for September 18. A month later they met again at the opera, and out of this meeting rose the proposal that Leonard should rent the top floor of the house at 38 Brunswick Square which Virginia and Adrian were planning to share with Maynard Keynes and Duncan Grant. Leonard moved from his mother's house to Brunswick Square on December 4, and from this end of the telescope it would appear that the outcome was obvious. Not so at the time.

There were four elements that made the result doubtful, and produced an unusually harrowing courtship. First, there was the problem of health. On Leonard's side, in the period September to December 1911 he had consulted several doctors about the inherited nervous tremor which made his hands shake so violently that on occasion he had had to adjourn court in Ceylon before he could gain sufficient composure to sign his name to judicial papers. Thoby Stephen had described Leonard to his sister as 'a man who trembled perpetually all over' and one night had 'dreamt he was throttling a man and dreamt with such violence that when he woke up he had pulled his own thumb out of joint'—a picture not wholly reassuring to a prospective bride. On Virginia's side, there was the history of mental instability which manifested itself at the end of January 1912 when she took to her bed with what she described to Leonard as 'a touch of my usual disease, in the head, you know'. Two

---

* Indeed it seems probable that Leonard had seen Virginia only four times: at the Trinity May Ball which she attended with Thoby in 1900; in the following year when Virginia and Vanessa visited Thoby's rooms in Trinity; on November 17, 1904 when Leonard dined with the Stephens before sailing for Ceylon; and at the Bells' on July 3, 1911.

weeks later this developed into a breakdown sufficiently serious to put her into a nursing home where, as she wrote Leonard, the inmates elected her King of the lunatics. It is not surprising that before his final proposal Leonard arranged to see Virginia's doctor, George Savage, a recognised authority on mental disorder and a friend of the Stephen family, who had attended Virginia since the earlier breakdown following the death of her father in 1904. We do not know what was said at this consultation, but the meeting itself on March 21, 1912, was recorded in Leonard's diary by means of a personal cypher of his own design which he had begun to use on December 8, 1911, four days after he had moved to Brunswick Square.

Then there was the smaller matter of other loves and lovers. Walter Lamb was still pursuing Virginia in a pathetically tenacious way, and in November 1911 a more vigorous suitor, Sydney Waterlow, had made his declaration to her. Virginia solved the Waterlow problem five days after Leonard moved into 38 Brunswick Square by telling Waterlow that she could not love him. But Leonard himself had a slight involvement. Since his return from Ceylon he had been seeing a good deal of a young lady whose family were close friends of the Woolfs—it is possible that Leonard was not prepared to give her up until he knew how matters with Virginia were going to turn out.

Third, was the cultural gap between the Woolf and Stephen families: not the difference between Reformed Jew and Agnostic Christian, but that between the professional middle class and the cultured and leisured upper class intellectual.

Finally, there was the really substantial problem of temperaments, which nearly proved the insurmountable obstacle to the match and about which a good deal must be said. In the novel Leonard later wrote about their courtship the difference in temperament is a major factor. A long list of differences in temperament between Leonard and Virginia could be developed; the one that 'counted' in this instance, and which continued to play a vital part throughout the lives of these two people, stemmed from what might be termed the double aspect of love. Love includes both the affirmative desire to love others and the more passive desire to be loved *by* others. Most people, presumably, have a quantity of each characteristic, but quite often in unequal proportions. Lytton Strachey, for example, 'was throughout his life always hopelessly in love or hopeless at not being in love'. He aggressively pursued love. He did not have an equally strong desire to be loved, placing a surprisingly low value on Dora Carrington's devotion to him. Virginia was nearly the opposite. She had a well defined desire to be loved by others but a very slight desire to love. Those for whom Virginia had strong affections fell within a narrow pattern of people occupying peculiarly supportive positions in relation to her: her father and mother; her elder brother Thoby and her elder sister Vanessa. Her affection for Clive Bell increased when he married Vanessa (and that is when Virginia had her most active flirtation with him and sought his literary guidance), but her feeling for Clive, both as an individual and as a literary adviser, diminished significantly when he was displaced in Vanessa's affections by Roger Fry in 1911. Virginia loved Vanessa's children, who were devoted to her, but had no comparable affection for the children of her younger brother, Adrian. Virginia's two youthful crushes—Madge Vaughan and Violet Dickinson (both considerably older than her)—occupied the same supportive positions as those members of her family to whom she was particularly attached. The mother figure dominated Virginia's thoughts most of her life. 'Until I was in the forties', she wrote, 'the presence of my mother obsessed me.' Virginia's interest in Madge Vaughan began a few years after the death of Julia Stephen. Virginia called Madge 'Mama' and 'foster parent', and asked that she be 'treated like a nice child'. In her letters to Violet Dickinson, Virginia frequently described herself as a baby kangaroo (what the Australians call a 'joey') who desires to crawl back into the pouch of its mother. As for Vita Sackville-West, Virginia's adult crush, she wrote that Vita 'lavishes on me the maternal protection which, for some reason, is what I have always most wished for from everyone. What L. gives me, and Nessa gives me and Vita, in her more clumsy external way, tries to give me.' In a majority of Virginia's novels either there is a motherless girl (*The Voyage Out, Night and Day, Mrs Dalloway* and *The Waves*) or the mother dies during the course of the story (*To the Lighthouse* and *The Years*). Even when it came to animals, Virginia's affection followed a similar one-way pattern which Quentin Bell thought 'odd and remote'. She 'nearly always had a dog', but she was not a dog lover. Significantly, in her relations with many of her closest friends she viewed herself as an animal—an object to be loved and cared for.* By contrast, Leonard, despite his reserve and his detachment, had both the desire to love and the desire to be loved in good measure.

---

* Quentin Bell says: 'In all her emotional relationships she pictured herself as an animal; to Vanessa she was a goat or sometimes a monkey, sometimes even a cartload of monkeys—*les singes*; to Violet Dickinson she was half monkey, half bird—Sparroy; to Leonard she was—surprisingly enough—Mandrill (and he Mongoose); to Vita she was Potto (a cocker spaniel, I think). These animal *personae*, safely removed from human carnality and yet cherished, the recipients indeed of hugs and kisses, were most important to her, but important as the totem figure is to the savage.' 2 QB 175–6.

Lytton was not wrong when he wrote to Leonard in 1909 that Virginia was 'longing to be in love'. She wanted, intellectually, to love 'vehemently', but it was not in her nature to do so. She was very straightforward about it: 'As I told you brutally the other day', she wrote to Leonard, 'I feel no physical attraction in you. There are moments— when you kissed me the other day was one—when I feel no more than a rock.' She adds, it is important to note, 'yet your caring for me as you do almost overwhelms me.'

The heroine of Leonard's novel *The Wise Virgins* says 'it's the voyage out that seems to me to matter, the new and wonderful things. I can't, I won't look beyond that. I want them all. I want love, too, and I want freedom. I want children even. But I can't give myself; passion leaves me cold.' Leonard also wrote a personal description of Virginia— apparently during the period of courtship—which was never published and which probably was never even shown by Leonard to anyone but the person to whom it was addressed. Virginia appears in it as 'Aspasia',* the name used for her in Leonard's diaries:

I am in love with Aspasia ... When I think of Aspasia I think of hills, standing very clear but distant against a cold blue sky; there is snow upon them which no sun has ever melted & no man has ever trodden. But the sun too is in her hair, in the red & the gold of her skin, in the bow of her lips & in the glow of her mind. And most wonderful of all is her voice which seems to bring things from the centre of rocks, deep streams that have lain long in primordial places beneath the earth. To drink once is to be intoxicated for ever. Whether she is walking or sitting there is always about her an air of quiet & clearness, but to think of her is to see her sitting, lying back in immense chairs before innumerable fires ...

I see her sitting among it all untouched in her quietness & clearness rather silent a little aloof & then the spring bubbles up—is it wit or humour or imagination? I do not know but the thought has come from strange recesses, life for a moment seems to go faster, you feel for a moment the blood in your wrists, your heart beat, you catch your breath as you do on a mountain when suddenly the wind blows. The things that come are strange often fantastic, but they are beautiful & always seem somewhere far below to have touched even to have been torn from reality. Perhaps this is because her mind is so astonishingly fearless, there is no fact & no reality which it does not face, touch frankly openly. She is one of possibly three women who know that dung is merely dung, death death & semen semen. She is the most Olympian of the Olympians. And that is why perhaps she seems to take life too hardly. She does not really know the feeling—which alone saves the brain & the body—that after all nothing matters. She asks too much from the earth & from the people

* 'Menexenus: Truly Socrates, I marvel that Aspasia, who is only a woman, should be able to compose such a speech, she must be a rare one.' Jowett, *The Dialogues of Plato,* vol. II p. 532.

who crawl about it. I am always frightened that with her eyes fixed on the great rocks she will stumble among the stones.

'And her heart?' you ask. Sometimes I think she has not got one, that she is merely interested in what will happen & in reality, that she is made merely of the eternal snow & the rocks which form the hidden centre of reality. And then I swear that this cannot be true, that the sun in her comes from a heart.*

We know Virginia's reaction to this because of comments added by Leonard:

I showed Aspasia her character as I had written it. She read it slowly in front of the fire. I forgot that she was reading it in the pleasure of watching her face & her hair: she must have sat silent thinking for some time when I heard her say: 'I don't think you have made me soft or lovable enough.'

Virginia did so earnestly want to be 'lovable'. As her niece Angelica Garnett put it 'She was ... avid for affection from those she loved'. And this desire to be lovable is expressed time after time in her letters. Her appearance of aloofness and independence was misleading. Actually she, like her father, desperately needed the constant support and protection of one whose devotion was unquestioned. Leonard was in so many respects qualified to fill this role, in big ways and little. His diary for January 7, 1912 reports: 'Did Virg's a/cs [accounts] with her'. His letter to her of May 24, 1912 begins 'Dearest and most beloved of all creatures!'

When, five days after this letter was written, Virginia told Leonard that she 'loved' him, she meant that she did so to the best of her capacity. More than anything else it was a reflection of the fact that she believed he truly loved her. And Leonard, on marriage, entered the hallowed circle, the narrow pattern of those on whom she could depend for unquestioning support, those with whom she felt most secure; in brief, those who loved her the most. Years later, 'probably between '30 and '36', Virginia while talking to an old friend 'said—and as though addressing herself rather than me: "What do you think is probably the happiest moment in one's whole life?" While I was wondering how I should answer this sudden question, she went on, with a strange but very quiet radiance in her voice: "I think its the moment when one is walking in one's garden, perhaps picking off a few dead flowers, and suddenly one thinks: My husband lives in that house—And he loves me." Her face shone, as I had never seen it.'

Not 'my husband lives in that house–and *I love him*',' but 'he loves me'. The importance of being loved by Leonard grew rather than diminished over the years.

* Virginia's diary entry for June 22, 1937 reads: 'I would like to write a dream story about the top of a mountain. Now why? About lying in the snow; about rings of colour; silence; and the solitude.' AWD 283.

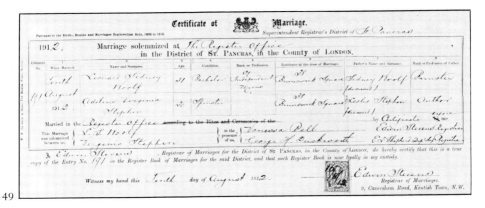

49

50

51

52

53

49 *Leonard and Virginia's marriage certificate. Presumably the phrase*
'of independent means' reflected Leonard's social status rather than his financial
condition. He had given up his job in Ceylon and his total net worth was £700, of
which £690 represented winnings in the Calcutta sweepstake

Scenes at Asheham. **50** *Virginia and Roger Fry.* **51** *Virginia and Ka Cox.*
52 *Leonard standing at corner of terrace.* **53** *Virginia with her dog.*

54 *Madge Symonds, who married Virginia's cousin William Vaughan, with their four children. Madge, 13 years older than Virginia, had been Virginia's first youthful crush*

55 *Violet Dickinson, 17 years older than Virginia and 6′ 2″ in her stockinged feet, was Virginia's second youthful crush*

56 *Leonard at Asheham with Adrian Stephen*

57 *with G. E. Moore*

58 *with dog*

59 *with Vanessa and Virginia*

Virginia's conclusion on May 29, 1912 that she loved Leonard and would marry him was a secret between the two for four days until Vanessa returned to London, and then, after she had been told, was promptly communicated to their friends in ways most congenial to the prospective bride and groom. Leonard wrote to G. E. Moore that 'I feel I should like to tell you myself that I am going to marry Virginia Stephen and that I'm extraordinarily happy. When you know her as I hope you will, I don't think you will be surprised.' Virginia wrote to Violet Dickinson that she was going to marry 'a penniless Jew'. A joint note to Lytton Strachey simply read:

> Ha! Ha!
> Virginia Stephen
> Leonard Woolf

It is not known how the news was conveyed to George Duckworth, Virginia's half-brother, but presumably it was less specific than the message to Violet Dickinson, since Duckworth wrote to Leonard suggesting that 'some formal arrangement should be made' for a settlement on Virginia, at the same time assuring Leonard that 'Virginia will be a most adorable wife'. The rejected Walter Lamb, one of the first to hear of the engagement, nobly wrote to Leonard: 'You have the love of the finest person I know of in the world.'

The marriage took place at the St Pancras Register Office on August 10. Virginia was 30 years old; Leonard a year older. Immediately after the wedding they left on a long honeymoon that began with a week in Sussex and Somerset followed by seven weeks in France, Spain and Italy, for which Leonard had withdrawn £105 from his bank account. After their return to England on October 3 they moved into rooms in Clifford's Inn, off Fleet Street, where 'a daily char came in and made the beds, swept up the smuts, and washed up the dishes'. Evening meals were taken at the nearby 'Cock Tavern'. Virginia continued with the work she most wanted to do—the completion of *The Voyage Out*. Leonard had terminated his job in the Ceylon Civil Service before Virginia had promised to marry him. Friends in Ceylon shipped Leonard's books to England and sold his few other possessions. After the honeymoon he took on various temporary jobs, first acting as Secretary to Roger Fry's Second Post-Impressionist Exhibition at the Grafton Galleries; then doing some work for the Charity Organisation Society and the Women's Co-operative Guild; and finally making a more permanent connection at the *New Statesman* where he began reviewing books on war and international affairs. All was not well, however.

Virginia complained of headaches and insomnia. Leonard started to keep a daily record of her health on January 13, 1913. Several doctors were consulted. On September 9, less than a year after the conclusion of their honeymoon, Virginia attempted suicide by taking a lethal dose of veronal.*

The delicate balance between sanity and insanity which was a part of Virginia's nature had been disrupted by several events. First, was the marriage itself. Apparently it had been consummated in a legal sense, but Virginia, 'made merely of the eternal snow', derived no pleasure from the sexual act and this must have occasioned some degree of tension between herself and Leonard, no matter how understanding he may have been. This, presumably, was what she referred to when she wrote to Leonard on August 4, 1913: 'Nothing you have ever done since I knew you has been in any way beastly—how could it be? You've been absolutely perfect to me. Its all my fault.' And on the following day: 'Dearest, I have been disgraceful—to you, I mean.' Virginia was increasingly conscious of her abnormality. This feeling was augmented by the decision of various doctors that she should not have children, another distinction between herself and Vanessa. Finally, there was the book: Virginia's novel. She had worked on it for at least six years, drafting and redrafting it again and again; Leonard thought it had been rewritten as many as ten or twenty times. It had finally been delivered to the publishers on March 9, 1913 and accepted on April 12. Virginia's headaches and sleeplessness began as the last changes were made before the manuscript was delivered to the publishers, and the symptoms returned, with incidents of depression, as the proofs were delivered to her and the date of publication approached. The depression was accompanied by delusions and increased resistance to eating. Three doctors were consulted, including Dr Savage. Rest and food were prescribed. Virginia went into a nursing home and from there she wrote the most endearing letters to Leonard: 'I want you Mongoose, and I do love you, little beast, if only I weren't so appallingly stupid a mandril.** Can you really love me—yes, I believe it, and we will make a happy life. You're so lovable.' After release from the nursing home she and Leonard went off for a holiday at Holford, Somerset, where they had spent the first part of their honeymoon. They returned to London in September. And then came the suicide attempt. Publication of *The Voyage Out* was deferred.

---

* Leonard incorrectly places the suicide attempt two years later—in 1915 (3LW 77).
** Mandril, ordinarily spelled with two ls, is described by the *Oxford English Dictionary* as 'The largest, most hideous, and most ferocious of the baboons'.

The remainder of 1913 and most of 1914 were devoted to Virginia's recovery. She spent two months with day and night nurses at George Duckworth's country house, Dalingridge Place at Tye's Cross, Sussex, and another three months with two nurses at Asheham, the Woolf country home in Sussex. It is not surprising that by March 1914 Leonard began to suffer from severe headaches and went off for a short visit to Lytton Strachey in Wiltshire. He wrote to Virginia every day; his letters were filled with assurances of his affection for her: 'I'm lonely without you. You can't realize how utterly you would end my life for me if you had taken that sleeping mixture successfully.' Later in the year, as Virginia improved, they made visits together to Hampstead, Cornwall and Northumberland.

In October 1914 they gave up their rooms in Clifford's Inn and moved to lodgings in Richmond. When it appeared that Virginia had fully recovered, a new publication date was set for *The Voyage Out*: March 26, 1915. But the symptoms of mental breakdown recurred. Virginia became excited and violent, and had to be moved to a nursing home. In the meanwhile Leonard had taken possession of Hogarth House in Richmond, to which Virginia was transferred with four nurses. There she stayed for four months. Several additional months were spent at Asheham, with a nurse and two servants. The nurse did not leave until November 1915, and by January 1916 Virginia was again leading a fairly normal life. Despite the presence of other factors, it is difficult not to conclude that the headaches, sleeplessness, and suicidal depression of 1913, together with the episodes of 1915, were primarily the result of a single cause: the publication of *The Voyage Out*, and that they represented the hysteria of a highly sensitive writer, always close to the edge of sanity, fearful that she would be 'found out' and adjudged mad by insensitive critics. In the event, the critics were not unkind to *The Voyage Out*. E. M. Forster found that it had attained 'the unity' of *Wuthering Heights*. Other critics hailed the book as the work of a genius. But by the time the reviews appeared Virginia was too ill to read them. One wonders whether the madness of 1915 might not have been wholly avoided if the publishers had released *The Voyage Out* in 1913 as originally planned, instead of deferring it to 1915 and thereby subjecting Virginia to two separate periods of harrowing anxiety.

The principal feature of Virginia's ravings during her mad spells was criticism of others—of men in general, of Leonard in particular, of ... for example ... the poetry of Frances Cornford. 'She says the most malicious and cutting things she can think of to everyone and they are so clever that they always hurt,' wrote Vanessa. It seems possible that this criticism of others was stimulated by her fear of what the critics would do to her.

Leonard was a practical and intelligent observer, and out of the horrors of 1913–15 he developed, no doubt with the advice of the doctors, a protective regimen that he successfully applied for the rest of Virginia's life: she must not get too excited; she must eat well and avoid any serious loss of weight; she must get plenty of rest and not be allowed to become unduly tired. One safeguard against excitement and becoming tired was leaving Clifford's Inn for Richmond, ten miles from Blooms-bury, where Leonard and Virginia lived from 1914 to 1924. Leonard prescribed bed hours and rest periods for Virginia. He limited Virginia's visitors and visiting to an extent that some of her friends thought tyrannical. He also saw to it that Virginia should have no excuse for not eating. In 1917, for example, £232 was spent on food, nearly a third of their total expenditure for the year. Leonard carefully watched what Virginia ate and weighed her regularly, entering the results in his diary. Between October 1, 1913 and October 14, 1915 her weight increased from 8 stone 7 pounds to 12 stone 7 pounds–a gain of nearly 50 per cent! Photographs taken of Virginia about the time she reached this peak show her as surprisingly plump. After her recovery in 1915 her weight was allowed to fall to the more normal level of something over 9 stone. For ten years following the suicide attempt, Leonard kept records of Virginia's menstrual periods, presumably because of the possibility that her mental disorders coincided with the occurrence of an unusually long interval between periods.* Today it is well recognised that there is a direct relationship between weight and menstruation, and that rejection of food may be a sign of sexual conflict–i.e. a rejection of femininity. An incident that occurred in 1917, involving elements of excitement, food and rest, illustrates Leonard's protective care. Barbara Hiles was having lunch with the Woolfs during the printing of Katherine Mansfield's *Prelude*; she and Virginia were giggling together when sud-denly Virginia began mischievously flicking meat off her plate in Bar-bara's direction. Leonard reprimanded Barbara for exciting Virginia (although she was not conscious of having done so) and led Virginia by the hand to her room, where she could lie down. At tea-time Virginia re-appeared, completely composed. In addition to this regulated system of life, Leonard provided another essential ingredient that Virginia needed

---

* In 1913 there was a 98 day interval between periods (from August 6 to November 12) when Virginia's weight fell to its lowest recorded level. Virginia was then extremely ill, and under the care of four nurses. There is no indication that she was pregnant.

as much as calm, nourishment and rest—namely, reassurance. Virginia was well aware of her mental instability. She also knew that her creative writing tended more and more to depart from literary convention. This did not worry her; what did worry her was whether she was writing sense or nonsense, and because of her history of madness she had frequent doubts as to her own judgment. 'Now what *will* they say about *Jacob*?' appears in Virginia's diary for June 23, 1922. 'Mad, I suppose: a disconnected rhapsody; I don't know.' But she greatly valued Leonard's judgment, and his appraisal of her manuscripts prior to publication provided some degree of certainty that her work would be accepted as sane. Thus Leonard became doctor, nurse, parent, semi-husband and chief literary adviser. And Leonard was a truly sympathetic critic; in an essay entitled 'Poetry & Prose' written years earlier when he was a boy at St Paul's, he had declared, 'I fail to see why a novel cannot be as poetical [as] a great many poems'.

Although Virginia had various illnesses after 1915, no serious counterpart of the 1913–15 experience occurred for the next 24 years—persuasive evidence of the efficacy of Leonard's system and the rigour of its enforcement. Indeed, in that 24-year period, the interruptions to Virginia's work due to problems of health did not greatly differ from what the average woman might have experienced in the same period. In four years out of the 24 she was ill for three days or less during the entire year; in ten years of the 24 she was ill for ten days or less during the year; and in only one year was she ill for more than three months. In total, her days of illness amounted to 7·5 per cent of the period, as compared with about 5 per cent for the average working woman in Great Britain during the 1970s, when modern antibiotics were available for the treatment of disease. Such figures, of course, provide only the crudest sort of evidence, yet Virginia's own diaries (which generally reflect more illness than Leonard records) may actually tend to overstate the case. Her diary shows that on April 8, 1936, after sending her manuscript of *The Years* to the printer, she 'collapses into bed and remains at Rodmell for a month, able to do nothing'. Leonard's diary records that Virginia had a headache on April 5, and that is all. It also shows that Leonard and Virginia played bowls on three days in April after the 8th, and records walks nearly every day with a visit to Charleston and a return visit by Vanessa, Clive, Angelica and Quentin. One does not know how seriously to take Vita Sackville-West's remark to Clive Bell that Virginia was '*such* a liar about her own health that one doesn't know what to believe; but Leonard (a saner and more truthful barometer) seemed optimistic'. Although Bloomsbury had consciously cast off most of the illusions of Victorianism, it had not purged itself of the nineteenth-century belief that illness is a spiritual virtue. The letters that passed between Bloomsbury friends are filled with references to ill health, very much in the tradition of their antecedents. How often at the Stephen breakfast table had they heard such plaintive notes as found their way into a 1896 letter from the painter G. F. Watts (he lived to be 87) to Leslie Stephen: 'I am a very poor creature myself, not a fortnight lately has passed without a day fretting in bed!' After all, Virginia herself had stated in her diary, 'I believe these illnesses are in my case—how shall I express it?—partly mystical'. And one cannot help noting the nine-year cycle of the principal attacks: 1895, 1904 and 1913 with a desperate (but successful) struggle against a breakdown in 1922 and now, in 1930—the date of the diary entry—another nine-year interval less than twelve months away.

Virginia's illnesses during these 24 years of relative good health were, in large measure, of the type most people experience. In more than half of the years she had a cold or influenza in December, January or February. She also had a number of toothaches and teeth were extracted one, two or three at a time until by the mid-30s she had few of her own left, and became more sensitive than ever about having her picture taken or posing for a portrait. The unusual illnesses occurred when Virginia was finishing a book. Then she commonly experienced periods of depression.* In letters to Frank Fish, Professor of Psychology at the University of Liverpool, written in 1966, Leonard stated: 'Virginia was normally in ordinary everyday life a happy person, very amusing, and frequently gay.' Again 'Normally, my wife was no more depressed or elated than the normal, sane person. That is to say that for 24 hours of, say 350 days in the year she was not more depressed or elated than I was or the "ordinary person".' When signs of depression did occur, Leonard's regimen went into operation almost automatically: food and rest were ordered; social life was restricted. Virginia simply disappeared. For this reason, many people who knew her well never saw any evidence of her intermittent melancholy. Lady Oxford wrote: 'I never knew till after her death that she ever had a mental breakdown. With me, she always appeared gay, happy and balanced.' Elizabeth Robins, the first English Hedda Gabler, who had known Virginia since her childhood, said, 'Virginia in my grateful memory is always smiling'. Professor William A.

---

* Samuel Butler, author of *The Way of All Flesh*, sometimes heard noises in his head on the point of going to sleep. 'When they show signs of returning', he said, 'I know it to be time to slacken off work', *The Family Letters of Samuel Butler 1841–1886* (1962) p. 221.

60

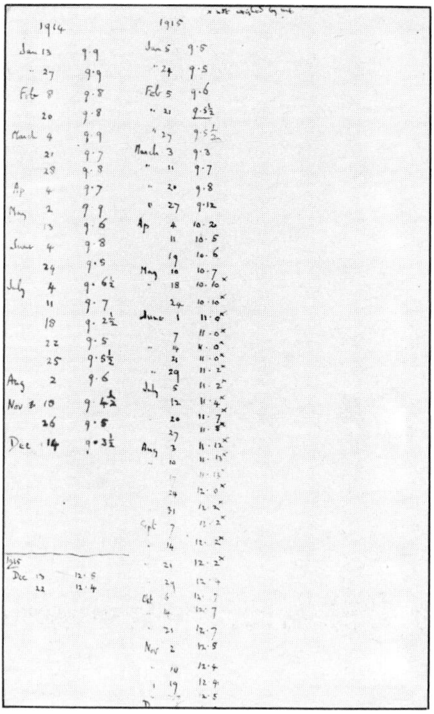

x not weighed by me

1914		1915	
Jan 13	9.9	Jan 5	9.5
" 27	9.9	" 24	9.5
Feb 8	9.8	Feb 5	9.6
20	9.8	" 21	9.5½
March 4	9.9	" 27	9.5½
21	9.7	March 3	9.3
28	9.8	" 11	9.7
Ap 4	9.7	" 20	9.8
May 2	9.9	" 27	9.12
13	9.6	Ap 4	10.2
June 4	9.8	11	10.5
24	9.5	19	10.6
July 4	9.6½	May 10	10.7x
11	9.7	" 18	10.10x
18	9.2½	24	10.10x
22	9.5	June 1	11.0x
25	9.5½	7	11.0x
Aug 2	9.6	" 14	11.0x
Nov 10	9.4½	21	11.0x
26	9.8	" 29	11.2x
Dec 14	9.3½	July 5	11.2x
		12	11.4x
		20	11.7x
		27	11.8x
		Aug 3	11.12x
		" 10	11.13x
		[illegible]	11.13x
		24	12.0x
		31	12.2x
		Sept 7	12.2x
		" 14	12.2x
		" 21	12.2x
		29	12.4
		Oct 6	12.7
		" 14	12.7
		" 21	12.7
		Nov 2	12.8
		" 10	12.4
		" 19	12.4
		[illegible]	12.5

1915	
Dec 13	12.5
22	12.4

61

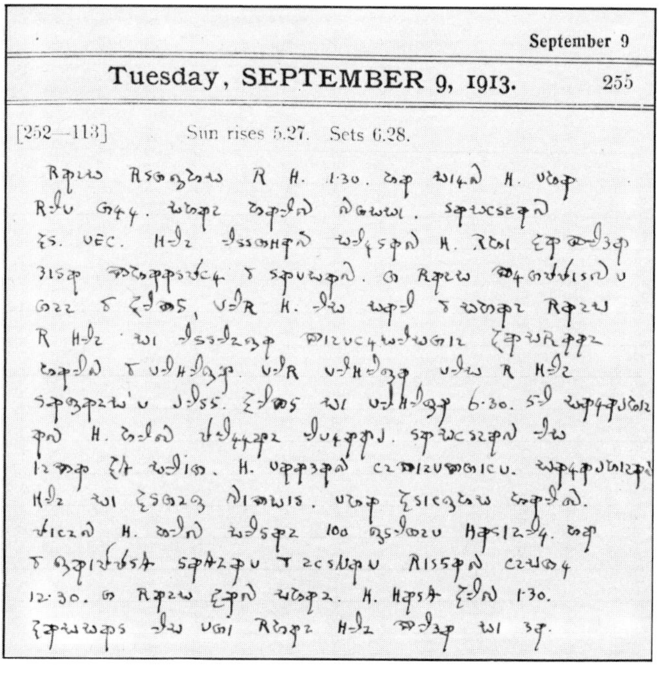

September 9

Tuesday, SEPTEMBER 9, 1913. 255

[252—113] Sun rises 5.27. Sets 6.28.

62

60 *Lily and Anny, two of Virginia's nurses*

61 *On September 30, 1913, three weeks after her suicide attempt, Virginia weighed 8 stone 7 pounds. Leonard's tabulation shows that she had gained more than a stone by January 13, 1914, and put on another three stone by the end of 1915 – a gain of roughly 60 pounds in a little more than two years*

62 *In 1911, after his return from Ceylon, Leonard created a code using Sinhalese and Tamilese symbols for the English alphabet in which he made diary entries that he wanted to keep confidential. The above entry that he made for September 9, 1913, reads:* Went Wright w V. 11.30. He told V. she was ill. Then Head ditto. Returned Br.Squ. Van arrived talked V. who became more cheerful & rested. I went Cliffords Inn & back. Saw V. at tea & then went w Van to arrange consultation between Head and Savage. Saw Savage Sat w Van Regents Park. Back to Savage 6.30. Ka telephoned V. had fallen asleep. Returned at once by taxi. V. seemed unconscious. Telephoned Van to bring doctor. She brought Head. Found V. had taken 100 grains Veronal. He & Geoffrey Keynes & nurses worked until 12.30. I went bed then. V. very bad 1.30. Better at six when Van came to me.

63 *Virginia, still weighing over 12 stone, went to Cornwall in 1916 with Leonard and Margaret Llewelyn Davies. Years later she wrote, 'unless I weigh 9½ stones I hear voices and see visions and can neither write nor sleep.'*

64 *Leonard and Margaret Llewelyn Davies*

Robson, whose association with Leonard Woolf began in 1927 at the founding of the *Political Quarterly*, has stated that Virginia always seemed 'brilliant and cheerful'. Virginia's nephew and biographer, Quentin Bell, who was 30 years old at the time of Virginia's death in 1941 and a frequent visitor at both Monks House and the Woolf home in Bloomsbury, has said that he never saw Virginia in a depressed mood. Moreover, Virginia thought of herself as an unusually happy person: 'I think perhaps 9 people out of ten never get a day in the year of such happiness as I have almost constantly.'

To sum up, it can fairly be said that while Virginia's health had to be watched carefully, there is little reason to conclude that during her most productive years—that is, between 1916 and 1940—her work was seriously curtailed by illness. On the other hand, there is good reason to believe that if Leonard Woolf had not regulated Virginia's life as he did, many of her works would have been lost to the world.

[6]

CAREERS:
YEARS OF ANXIETY

65 *Virginia*

When Virginia and Leonard married they decided they would support themselves by writing. Leonard had completed a novel of native life in Ceylon but also wanted 'to find out about labour and factories'. Apparently this was not visualised as a source of income since he intended 'to keep outside Government and do things on his own account'.

Leonard's account books show that on their wedding day, August 10, 1912, Virginia had 'capital' (i.e. investments in securities and other property) of £9,013. 16s. 9d. and a bank balance of £30. 12s. 11d. Leonard at September 10 had 'capital' of £506 1s. 0d. and a balance in the bank, after drawing out funds for their honeymoon, of £14 7s. 8d. The annual income from Virginia's investments, according to Leonard, was 'rather less than £400'.

Their plans were to 'take a small house and try to live cheaply, so as not to have to make money'. No records have been found of their expenditure in the first two years of married life, but there is a tabulation in Leonard's diary for 1915 which appears to be a budget for the year prepared at the end of 1914 or early in 1915 when they were living in rooms at Richmond. It adds up to £443. At this level of expenditure very little earned income would be required to cover living costs. The twelve guineas a month that Leonard received from the first job he took after he was married—temporary employment as Secretary for Roger Fry's Second Post-Impressionist Exhibition—would have been adequate to cover their needs.

Virginia's illness in the early years changed these prospects. Quite apart from the cost of doctors, nurses and nursing homes, it was clear after the recurrence of her mental breakdown in the spring of 1915 that they could not continue to live in rooms as contemplated in the 1915 budget, that they would have to have a house and servants, and that much more would have to be spent on food because of the need to keep Virginia's weight up and the added people that would have to be fed. Thus the Woolf budget for 1917 rose to £680. Two years later, when the Woolfs' lease expired at Asheham and they bought Monks House, their annual expenditure began to exceed £800. At this stage there was a gap of more than £400 between annual requirements and income from investments, a gap substantial enough to cause concern. At the outset, however, it seemed possible that their financial needs could be met by writing fiction. Leonard's novel *The Village in the Jungle* was to be published in February 1913. Virginia's novel *The Voyage Out*, as we have seen, was accepted by Duckworth two months later.

The Village in the Jungle was a remarkable first novel derived from Leonard's seven years of close association with the people of Ceylon. Acclaimed on publication, it was reprinted twice in 1913, again in 1925 and at various later dates; it is still in print and still being purchased and read. A letter from Alec Waugh to Leonard, written in 1965, explains the basis of its broad appeal:

A year ago when I was reading about 'The Village in the Jungle' in your auto-biography, I said to myself 'That's a book I've got to read', and a few weeks later in Singapore, I was saying to a young Malay student 'no Western novelist —not even Forster—has really got inside the Asian mind. Kipling and

66 *Leonard with Nehru in 1936*

CONFIDENTIAL.

[January 3, 1919.]

FOREIGN OFFICE.

P.C. 019.

INTERNATIONAL GOVERNMENT UNDER THE LEAGUE OF NATIONS.

PREFATORY NOTE.

I hope that this paper may be some use to the section dealing with the League of Nations at the Peace Conference. Most of it is not original. The facts contained in Part I are taken almost entirely from "International Government," by L. S. Woolf (1916). Where a mass of facts has been collected and sifted with great ability, as is the case with Mr. Woolf's work, it would be folly to attempt to do the work over again, especially when time presses. My detailed descriptions of the various existing organs of international government are therefore for the most part lifted almost verbatim, with slight abridgements, from Mr. Woolf's book. Only the arrangement is largely my own, and some of the suggestions for further international action, together with the skeleton of a possible comprehensive organisation under the League of Nations. Also in some small particulars I have been able to supplement Mr. Woolf's facts from official sources. It follows that I cannot guarantee the accuracy of details throughout ; but the character of Mr. Woolf's work is such that no serious inaccuracy need be feared.

If this paper is found useful its defects of omission and commission can be remedied, and it can be filled out with detail from official sources.

S. P. WATERLOW.

Foreign Office, December 28, 1918.

PART I.—*Existing Organs of International Government and their Extension.*

The individuals comprising states have, under modern conditions, a number of vital interests which cannot be satisfied by purely national action. Those interests are a direct consequence of the industrial revolution, which, by creating large scale industry, international trade, finance, and communications, changed the structure of human society. But to this change there has not corresponded an adequate development either of political ideals or of political organisation. The ideal of the "independent sovereign state" begotten by the renascence out of the Middle Ages still holds the field, although the facts have outgrown it ; and international organisation to fit the facts has been hampered by failure to perceive the discrepancy. The development of international government in the period 1830–1914 was remarkable indeed, but haphazard. The establishment of the League of Nations should now make it possible, not only to co-ordinate the existing piecemeal growths, but to extend international administration systematically to those further spheres of life in which it is urgently needed.

The present situation may be summarised as follows. The "independent sovereign states" have already, to a much greater extent than is commonly realised, consented to curtailments of their sovereignty* by treaties (1) subjecting their national interests to the control of international bodies created *ad hoc*, and (2) binding themselves to take uniform domestic measures. But they have only done this where the pressure of necessity has been grossly obvious. There remain many national interests which ought

* The word is used here only in a loose, non-technical sense.

[752]—5

B

67

To the Electors of the

Combined
University

English
Constituency.

I AM asking for your votes as a candidate adopted by the Seven Universities' Democratic Association. The general principles of the policy which I support are given in the programme of that Association, and upon it I take my stand. The Association is affiliated to the Labour Party, of which I have been a member for some considerable time. In asking you to vote for me I am, therefore, asking you to give your support to that Party, and I should like to say a word upon this point before giving in greater detail the policy which I would support if I were returned as your member. We have in this country two alternatives before us at this election: we can once more entrust the government of the country to one of the two political parties which, for the better part of a century, have separately or in coalition been in power, and which, therefore, are jointly and severally responsible for the social, political, economic, and international conditions in which we find ourselves to-day; on the other hand, we have an opportunity of making a break with the past and of entrusting the government to a party of new principles and of new men. I confess that one reason why I am a member of the Labour Party, and why, with some confidence, I ask you to support that Party by your vote, is this: that, looking round upon the political and economic conditions in London and Manchester, in Dublin, India, and Egypt, and remembering the graves in France and Gallipoli which were to be the price of a new world, I feel that this is no time for a mere reshuffle of the ancient Conservative and Liberal pack and for entrusting power to one or other of the two parties whose political principles and practice are directly responsible for the disastrous situation in which the Country finds itself to-day. A century of Conservative and Liberal Government brought us war and a peace which has proved

67 *The confidential Government report made by Sydney Waterlow which was based on facts from Leonard Woolf's* International Government

68 *Leonard's election address as a candidate for Parliament, October 1922*

69 *The information copied by Virginia in 1917 from Consular Reports for Leonard's book on international trade has its current interest since it shows that as early as 1891 Bordeaux was importing 45 million gallons of wine a year*

70 *The tabulation is an example of the many types of records kept by Leonard. It shows his progress in writing a book, in this instance* The War for Peace *published in 1940. The book was written between December 1939 and May 1940, and Leonard has recorded the number of words he wrote each day, beginning with 349 words on the first day and ending with 97 on the last, for a total of 61,649 words*

Maugham described the effect of the Far East on the Westerner'. The Malay said 'There is one novel that has. The Village in the Jungle.'

I have now kept my promise to myself and read your novel and I must send you a note to thank you for the pleasure you have given me. I was held and moved right the way through: the pace and force of the narrative are terrific. You have done what I did not think it was possible for a Westerner to do—got inside the mind and heart of the Far East. It is a unique achievement.

The financial rewards, however, were exceedingly modest. The publisher had printed a small initial edition and small follow-up editions so that the author's royalties, at 6d. per copy for the first 1,000 copies and 9d. thereafter, came to £63 in the first sixteen years of the book's life. But encouraged by the good reviews, Leonard felt that if he could get a second book promptly before the public both books would benefit. He was then working on a novel called *The Wise Virgins*. This was hurriedly completed and published in October 1914. It proved to be a disaster.

Its interest today is in its portrayal of character, since the principal actors are Leonard and Virginia. The story, although dealing with their courtship, has a different ending: the hero is forced to marry the girl next door, whom he has compromised. Leonard appears as Harry Davis, a young Jewish painter living with his family in Richstead. Virginia is represented by the beautiful, passionless Camilla Lawrence, also a painter, who lives with her wealthy father in London. She is bound by a 'curiously strong love' to her sister Katherine, a writer, who is described as being real 'flesh and blood'. The Davis culture is contrasted with the Lawrence culture: Woolf-Putney with Stephen-Bloomsbury, to the disadvantage of Putney. Leonard's family and their friends were so unsympathetically portrayed that Leonard's mother, after reading the manuscript, stated that if the novel was published as written 'I feel there will be a serious break between us'. Certain changes were made, but even in the published version Leonard's mother and his sister Bella are treated roughly. Leonard treats himself equally harshly: Harry Davis has a 'look of discontent, discomfort, almost suffering in his face' which is 'impassive, almost cruel'; he is a self-satisfied, cynical egoist, who is uneasy in company and does not get along with people. Leonard's sister Bella saw in Harry Davis all Leonard's 'less pleasant characteristics magnified to the nth power', adding that 'If you had made—or would make—Harry really yourself you would make a fine thing of him'. The anonymous reviewer in the *Times Literary Supplement* went farther than Bella: he not only found Harry Davis 'a most unpleasant young man', but thought that the group surrounding Camilla Lawrence one of 'those little coteries of depressed people who never seem to get anything worth having out of life'. Only a small first edition of *The Wise Virgins* had been printed and only a small part of this printing was sold. Leonard's total earnings from the book were £20. 'The war', Leonard later explained, 'killed it dead'. The book has never been reprinted and is extremely scarce. We know of only one copy that has been offered for sale in the past several years, and this was priced at £60.

Perhaps under other circumstances Leonard would have gone on to write a third novel if two events had not intervened. In the midsummer of 1913 Virginia had suffered the severe mental breakdown associated with the impending publication of *The Voyage Out* and then, after what appeared to be a period of recovery, there was the dreadful recurrence in 1915. This not only meant large bills, but also meant a substantial reduction of any revenue-producing work by Leonard, who took over the nursing of Virginia in the later stages of her illness. In the nine months from August 1914 to June 1915 Leonard's total earnings from journalism amounted to £17 7s. 6d. Medical bills in 1915 alone amounted to £500; the Woolfs had to sell some of their property—Virginia's jewellery and probably some securities—to pay these bills and to meet current living expenses.

The other event that occurred was a more fortunate one, since it opened up new avenues of interest and income for Leonard. Early in 1913, through the influence of Margaret Llewelyn Davies, 'who', according to Virginia, 'could compel a steam roller to waltz', Leonard had become interested in the co-operative movement, and in June, when he was in the process of completing *The Wise Virgins*, he made a trip to Newcastle to attend the annual congress of the Women's Co-operative Guild. His report of that meeting, printed in the *Manchester Guardian*, brought him to the attention of Beatrice and Sidney Webb, who invited the Woolfs to lunch on July 12, 1913 in order to determine whether Leonard was the type of bright young man they found useful. As it turned out, this luncheon meeting probably settled the pattern of Leonard's career. Most immediately, Sidney Webb, then Chairman of the *New Statesman*, introduced Leonard to the editor with a view to his being employed as a reviewer of books on war and foreign affairs, and his association with the *New Statesman* (except for an interval in the 1920s when he became Literary Editor of the *Nation*) lasted for half a century. Next, the Webbs persuaded Leonard to accept a commission to write two reports for the Fabian Society on the creation of an international authority for the peaceful settlement of disputes, a subject which continued of lifelong interest to him. Third, through the Webbs Leonard himself became a member of the Fabian Society, and he retained an active interest in it until his death. Finally, after Sidney Webb became a member of the Labour Party executive in 1917 he set up several advisory committees to assist Labour Party members of Parliament—one on international questions and another on imperial (colonial) questions. Leonard was made secretary of each of these, and served on them for 27 years.

The first of the two reports Leonard wrote for the Fabian Society was published in 1915 as a supplement to the *New Statesman*, and in 1916 both parts appeared in a book entitled *International Government* which subsequently played a significant role in the creation of those parts of the League of Nations, and later of the United Nations, that have proved most effective. 'In December 1918', wrote Philip Noel-Baker, 'when the Foreign Office was beginning to organise its League of Nations Section, the late Sydney Waterlow "discovered" Woolf's book *International Government*. Waterlow's enthusiasm was aroused; he condensed the book into a brilliant F.O. "print", laying emphasis on Woolf's vision of the scope for international co-operation over labour conditions, public health, transport, economic and social policy, etc. Lord (Robert) Cecil, the head of the section, was deeply impressed by the "print" and incorporated virtually the whole of Woolf's ideas into the British Draft Covenant which he gave to Woodrow Wilson in Paris.* Woolf thus played an important part in giving concrete form to the general ideas about a League then current, and in particular in launching the conception of the League's technical, social, economic and financial work, which has developed into a dozen U.N. Agencies, from the I.L.O. and the International Bank to the World Meteorological Organisation.'

The writing of *International Government* took place during Virginia's protracted illness. As we have seen, Virginia's first novel, *The Voyage Out*, did not ultimately appear until March 1915 and Virginia did not fully recover until the end of that year. *The Voyage Out*, superficially, was the story of a motherless girl, Rachel Vinrace, who travels to South America on a freighter, meets a young man with whom she falls in love, then contracts a tropical fever and dies. But as Virginia was later to say, 'every secret of a writer's soul, every experience of his life, every quality of his mind is written large in his works'. *The Voyage Out* is intensely autobiographical. The title of the book referred to Virginia's own

---

* A copy of *International Government* had also been sent by the U.S. Naval Headquarters in London to Colonel House, U.S. delegate to the Versailles Peace Conference and co-drafter of the League of Nations Covenant, with the comment that 'Mr. L. S. Woolf ... has collated in a most scholarly way, a mass of data carefully sifted of experiences and precedents for international government which may prove of use to you, as a scaffolding.'

voyage out from the backwater of Hyde Park Gate into the mainstream of life. The prototype of Rachel's boat trip was Virginia's own trip to Lisbon. Rachel's aunt and uncle, Mr and Mrs Ambrose, who accompany her on the trip, are derived from Virginia's father and mother. There is also something of Vanessa in Mrs Ambrose. Rachel's delirium during her fever is Virginia's delirium during one of her breakdowns. Bloomsbury is well represented. One of the young men in the story, St John Hirst, is modelled on Lytton Strachey. A copy of G. E. Moore's *Principia Ethica*–'a black volume of philosophy' (actually it was dark brown) lies on the table next to Mrs Ambrose. The ship is the *Euphrosyne* —the title of a book of puerile verse by Clive, Lytton, Saxon, Leonard and others, which they had published privately in 1905 and urgently wished to forget.

The critics liked the book. The *T.L.S.* reviewer found it 'clever and shrewd' with 'a quivering eagerness about life'. The characters were 'brilliantly drawn'. But when it came to the banal problem of covering living expenses, *The Voyage Out* was not much more successful than Leonard's *The Village in the Jungle*, earning an aggregate of only £120 over the next 15 years.

In 1916, when Virginia was finally restored to health, the Woolfs were still in a position that made it necessary to borrow or to dispose of capital to cover living costs. During the year they spent a total of £676 4s. 0d. Virginia's reviews for the *T.L.S.*, which averaged about one a month, could not have produced more than £35 in a year, at the rate then being paid. Leonard's earnings were £176: £50 from the Fabian Society for *International Government*, £1 18s. 3d. from royalties on his two novels, £2 2s. 0d. from a lecture, £21 from articles in the *Labour Leader*, £1 3s. 6d. from the sale of copies of books he had reviewed, and most of the balance from the *New Statesman* for articles and reviews in that periodical. Assuming about £300 income from what remained of Virginia's capital their expenses still exceeded their joint income by around £160.

The passage of the Military Service Act in 1916, with its provisions for conscription, had brought new anxieties. Although Leonard was 35, he was in danger of being called up. Two Harley Street doctors (Craig and Wright) who had been treating Leonard for years certified that he was unfit for service because of 'an inherited Nervous Tremor which is quite uncontrollable' and headaches that 'easily come on with fatigue'. Dr Craig, who had been consulted about Virginia's health, mentioned that Leonard had personally nursed Virginia through her mental breakdowns and stated that it would be highly detrimental to her health if

71

71-3 *Virginia was photographed by three of the great artists of the camera:
the Englishman, G. C. Beresford; the American, Man Ray; and the
Frenchwoman, Giselle Freund.*

85

72

These three pictures by Man Ray, taken when Virginia was about 45, have never been reproduced as a group

73

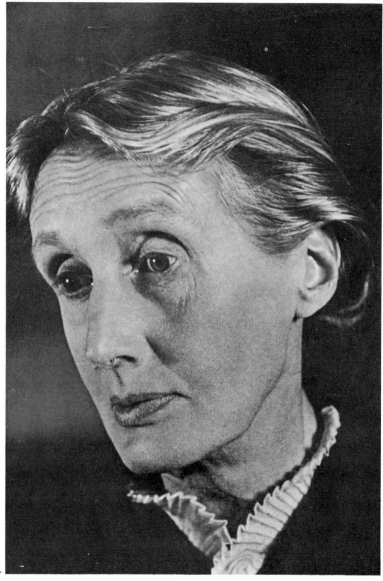

74

74–5 *Photographs by courtesy of Giselle Freund*
Most of the photographs of Virginia taken by Giselle Freund have been
reproduced many times. We have shown above only those that are not widely
known. These pictures were taken when Virginia was in her 50s

75

Leonard's care were removed. Happily, the decision of the Military Service Act Tribunal granted him exemption from military service on medical grounds, which removed another question mark from their lives. Virginia wrote to her friend Ka Cox: 'Leonard has been completely exempted from serving the Country in any capacity. He went before the military doctors trembling like an aspen leaf, with certificates to say he would tremble and has trembled and would never cease from trembling. It's a great mercy for us.'

Thus in 1917, the fifth year in the Woolfs' married life, both were able to work without serious interruption. Virginia applied herself to her second novel and wrote 33 reviews for the *Times Literary Supplement*, as well as doing a huge amount of dull copying work for Leonard in connection with a second book he had been commissioned to write for the Fabian Society. The Hogarth Press was founded and in its first year produced a profit, but only a tiny one of less than £7. Leonard increased his earnings to £241. Yet there was again a deficit and again a call on Virginia's capital. This pattern of periodic deficits and what appears to have been an annual diminution of capital continued for the next six years, and hence was a way of life from 1912 to 1923.* The income from Virginia's modest patrimony had shrunk to less than half its original sum by 1918–19, and to an even lower figure by 1921–2. We also know that at least in 1918, and perhaps other years as well, Virginia raised money by selling some books and manuscripts which she had inherited from her father. While Leonard, according to his autobiography, 'never worried' about money, Virginia 'every now and again ... would get into a sudden panic about our finances ... But the panic did not last and we took no immediate steps to find me a paid job.' Virginia had stated even before they were married: 'It seems idiotic to put Leonard into an office, for the sake of a bigger income'.

Virginia's second novel, *Night and Day*, was published in 1919. It was her counterpart to Leonard's *The Wise Virgins*. It, too, told of their courtship, the gap between the Stephen and Woolf cultures, and the character of the two principals—but in each case in a softer, less realistic way than Leonard's portrayal. Virginia's version was also far more humourous, particularly in the wonderfully amusing description of Mrs

---

* From December 1918 to the end of 1922 Leonard was employed as editor of a new monthly publication, *The International Review*, and then as editor of a 16-page international section of the *Contemporary Review*, while he continued his freelance work for other publications. For his editorial work he received £250 per annum in the first three years and £200 in the fourth. The figures on earnings and expenditures for this period are not complete and it is possible that during some of these years there was no deficit or only a small one.

76 *Virginia – a studio photograph*

77

78

77–9 *Virginia in the upstairs sitting room in Monks House*

80 *Virginia at Garsington, 1923, Lord David Cecil's head in foreground*

79

80

Hilbery—Virginia's Aunt, Annie Thackeray Ritchie. Apparently the Ritchies did not find the description so amusing, and they were furious with Virginia on account of it. It is possible too that Virginia was having a bit of fun with Leonard by calling her heroine 'Katherine' (modelled somewhat on Vanessa) and endowing her with a high level of mathematical skills, since Camilla's sister in *The Wise Virgins* was a Katherine 'who can't understand the binomial theorem'. The major difference, however, in the two novels is in their structure: Leonard wrote a story about specific individuals; Virginia used specific individuals to write about a universal theme: What is love? Is it 'a humorous sort of tenderness for him, a zealous care for his susceptibilities'? Is it 'only a story one makes up in one's mind about another person'? One is left with the impression that it may be any one of many things depending on the individual. To the sensitive, shy intellectual Katherine Hilbery, and presumably to Virginia, the answer seems to be found in the words: 'You've destroyed my loneliness'. This is not a casual observation. Lonely people appear in every Virginia Woolf novel, and we learn from them that loneliness can be destroyed by love, by work—or by death. The reviewer for the *Times Literary Supplement* found *Night and Day* full of wisdom and humour and 'so exciting that to read it is to pass through a keen emotional experience'.

In 1920 Leonard published another book of major importance: *Empire and Commerce in Africa*.* Of this, Philip Noel-Baker said: 'it stirred the conscience of the Colonial Powers, and evoked the sense of trusteeship for subject peoples'. In the following year Leonard's last work of fiction was published, a slim volume of 55 pages entitled *Stories from the East*. This contained three tales—probably written before—one of which ('Pearls and Swine'), according to the reviewer for the *Daily Mail* 'will rank with the great stories of the world'. When asked to sugar-coat this story so that it would be acceptable for the American market, Leonard declared he had no inclination to rewrite the story, and it has never been published in the United States.

Virginia's third novel, *Jacob's Room*, was published in 1922. It is a prose-poem written in memory of her adored brother Thoby, who had died sixteen years before when he was 26. 'It is love that alone gives life', wrote Samuel Butler, 'and the truest life is that which we live not in ourselves but vicariously in others ... ' The account of Jacob written by Virginia is largely the life he lived vicariously in others. Jacob himself

---

* Between *International Government* in 1916 and *Empire and Commerce in Africa* in 1920, Leonard had published *The Future of Constantinople* (1917) and *Co-Operation and the Future of Industry* (1918).

81

81 *Virginia in Monks House sitting room*
82 *The upstairs sitting room, Monks House, where most of the interior photographs were taken, as it is today*

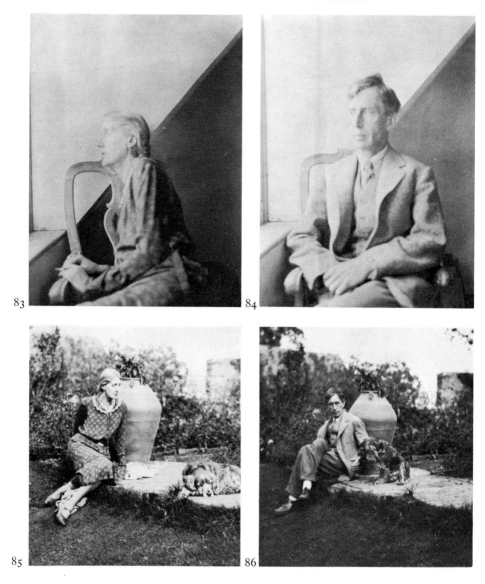

83–6 *Photographs taken in the upstairs sitting room and the garden of Monks House*

rarely speaks. The technique used by Virginia was new, and many of the critics of the day found it difficult. The life is not described in the orderly way in which biographers or traditional novelists arrange their subjects with balanced emphasis on each worldly attainment, but is set forth in what might seem to be a mass of disorganised and disjointed impressions, important and unimportant, such as are stored away, higgledy-piggledy, in the lumber room of our minds. The *Times Literary Supplement*, while applauding the 'adventurousness' of Virginia's method, concluded that 'it does not create persons and characters as we secretly desire to know them'. *Jacob's Room* was, however, liked by Virginia's critical friends: 'This time the reviews are against me and the private people enthusiastic.' Two editions totalling 2,200 were printed in England in 1922, and when issued in the United States in the following year, 2,500 copies were printed.

While Virginia was engaged in finishing *Jacob's Room*, Leonard was standing for Parliament. At that time, the English Universities had eight members in Parliament: two each from Oxford, Cambridge and London Universities and two from the Combined English University Constituency representing the seven other English universities. Leonard was asked to become a candidate by a group called the Seven Universities Democratic Association, which was affiliated with the Labour Party. His campaign, extending theoretically from May 1920 to the election in November 1922, was half-hearted; he spoke at only four of the seven universities included in the constituency, evoked no great enthusiasm among the electors, and as expected was unsuccessful—polling only 12 per cent of the vote.

Thus ended the first eleven years of married life, a period that included a world war and Virginia's long bout of insanity. The Woolfs had not quite managed to support themselves by writing. Their plans had been upset by Virginia's illness and the higher scale of living demanded by her health. Yet much had been accomplished in these years of anxiety. In what must be regarded as his most productive period, Leonard had written three distinguished books: *The Village in the Jungle, International Government*, and *Empire and Commerce in Africa*. Virginia had established herself as a writer, and although her most productive years lay ahead, those who knew her were confident of a brilliant future. What no one could have foreseen at the time was the extent of that future, or the growth of The Hogarth Press, which had been quietly founded in 1917.

THREE JEWS

By

LEONARD WOOLF.

It was a Sunday and the first day of spring, the first day on which one felt at any rate spring in the air. It blew in at my window with its warm breath , with its inevitable little touch of sadness . I felt restless, and I had nowhere to go to; everyone I knew was out of town. I looked out of my window at the black trees breaking into bud, the tulips and the hyacinths that even London could not rob of their reds and blues and yellows, the delicate spring sunshine on the asphalt, and the pale blue sky that the chimney pots broke into. I found myself muttering . "damn it" for no very obvious reason. It was spring, I suppose, the first stirring of the blood.

I wanted to see clean trees, and the sun shine upon grass; I wanted flowers and leaves unsoiled by soot; I wanted to see and smell the earth; above all I wanted the horizon. I felt that

18   THREE JEWS

"Dad, I want to marry a girl"—a really nice girl"—"but she's not one of us: will you give me your permission and blessing?" Well I don't believe in it. Our women are as good, better than Christian women. Aren't they as beautiful, as clever, as good wives? I know my poor mother, God rest her soul, used to say: "My son," she said, "if you come to me and say you want to marry a good girl, a Jewess, I don't care whether she hasn't a chemise to her back, I'll welcome her—but if you marry a Christian, if she's as rich as Solomon, I've done with you—don't you ever dare to come into my house again." Vell, I don't go as far as that, though I understand it. Times change: I might have received his wife, even though she was a Goy. But a servant girl who washed my dishes! I couldn't do it. One must have some dignity."

He stood there upright, stern, noble: a battered scarred old rock, but immovable under his seedy black coat. I couldn't offer him a shilling; I shook his hand, and left him brooding over his son and his graves.

THE MARK ON THE WALL

By

VIRGINIA WOOLF

Perhaps it was the middle of January in the present year that I first looked up and saw the mark on the wall. In order to fix a date it is necessary to remember what one saw. So now I think of the fire; the steady film of yellow light upon the page of my book; the three chrysanthemums in the round glass bowl on the mantelpiece. Yes, it must have been the winter time, and we had just finished our tea, for I remember that I was smoking a cigarette when I looked up and saw the mark on the wall for the first time. I looked up through the smoke of my cigarette and my eye lodged for a moment upon the burning coals, and that old fancy of the crimson flag flapping from the castle tower came into my mind, and I thought of the cavalcade of red knights riding up the side of the black rock. Rather to my relief the sight of the mark interrupted the fancy, for it is an old fancy, an automatic

[7]

THE HOGARTH PRESS

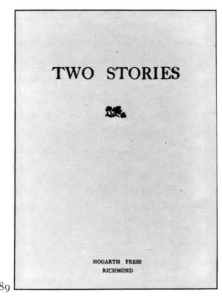

TWO STORIES

HOGARTH PRESS
RICHMOND

89

87–9 *Pages from* Two Stories

In 1917, while Leonard and Virginia were living in Richmond at Hogarth House, they bought a miniature printing press and a small quantity of type for a little over £19. Neither had any printing experience, but with the aid of a manual of instruction and several weeks of practice they produced a short announcement of their intention to print 'a pamphlet containing two stories' which they had written. Virginia's story was *The Mark on the Wall*; Leonard's, *Three Jews*. They invited subscriptions for the pamphlet at 1*s.* 6*d.*, to be paid in advance by postal order.

Although they found their new toy 'the most absorbing of all pursuits' it also proved time-consuming. It took them two months, working nearly every afternoon, to produce the 34-page pamphlet. The type purchased with the press was only sufficient to set up two small pages. After these had been inked and run off on the press, one sheet at a time, the formes had to be broken up so that the type could be used for the succeeding two pages. No one knows exactly how many copies were printed—Leonard estimated that it was about 150. What we do know is how many were sold. Leonard entered the date, the name (with one exception) of the purchaser, and the amount paid for each copy in one of his old account books left over from Ceylon. This record shows that about 100 copies were subscribed for prior to the date of publication in July 1917, and that 135 copies had been sold two years later when the pamphlet was presumably declared out of print. Most of those who purchased copies after the date of publication paid two shillings per copy, except for the unnamed purchaser of the 135th (and last) copy, who paid 7s. 6d.

Virtually all the copies of *Two Stories* were bought by friends and relations of the authors. The more notable among those (outside Bloomsbury) were John Drinkwater, Beatrice Webb, Mrs Bernard Shaw, Michael Sadler, Edward Garnett, William Rothenstein and Katherine Mansfield.

Publication No. 1 was in the hand-craft tradition of Roger Fry's Omega Workshops. It was illustrated with four woodcuts by Dora Carrington, an Omega artist, who was paid 15 shillings for her work. Its covers (until the supply ran out and plain yellow paper had to be substituted) were made of attractive blue and red Japanese grass paper. And like the handful of books published by the Omega Workshops beginning in 1915, it contained worthwhile material for which a commercial publisher probably could not have been found. But *unlike* Omega Workshops and hundreds of other artistic ventures, The Hogarth Press was profitable from the start. According to the meticulous accounts kept by Leonard, the Press cleared £6 7s. on its first publication, although nothing was charged for Leonard and Virginia's services either as author or printer. Encouraged by the profit, the Woolfs bought some more type and a guillotine in preparation for their next publication.

The second publication was more ambitious in every respect than the first. The text was much longer and the author, Katherine Mansfield, even more obscure. Type setting for her short story, *Prelude*, was started by Leonard and Virginia in November 1917. The 68 pages of this book took more than eight months to print. During that period Leonard

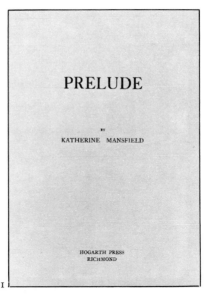

90–1 Prelude: *title page and cover showing decoration by J. D. Fergusson used only on the first few copies printed*

and Virginia worked on it nearly every afternoon, Virginia doing most of the type-setting and Leonard attending to the machining. The Hogarth Press hired its first outsider — Barbara Hiles — who for several months worked three days a week in return for her transportation, a noon-day meal ('meat, 2 veg and pudding'), and an unspecified share in the profits. Her total receipts came to £2 2s. 6d., inclusive of transportation, and one free copy of the book. *Prelude* was priced at 3s. 6d., and moved very slowly. From the date it was issued in July 1918 to the end of the year only 84 copies were sold; and it was not until 1923 that the book was declared out of print. The author's royalties from the book were £5 6s. 6d. The Hogarth Press profit, after these payments and other costs, including a small sum for advertising, amounted to a shade less than £16.

Although Katherine Mansfield's book was scheduled to be the second Hogarth Press publication, and is currently offered as such by antiquarian booksellers, it actually became the third through an unhappy circumstance. Early in December 1917, while in the midst of setting type for *Prelude*, news was received of the death of Leonard's brilliant younger brother Cecil, at the battle of Cambrai. Another brother, Philip, was seriously wounded by the same shell. When Philip was invalided home, Leonard put *Prelude* to one side and with the help of Virginia set the type for a handful of Cecil's poems. They printed for

POEMS

BY

C. N. SIDNEY WOOLF
LATE 20TH HUSSARS (SPEC. RES.)
FELLOW OF TRINITY COLLEGE, CAMBRIDGE

HOGARTH PRESS, RICHMOND
1918

92

Cecil Sidney Woolf was born on Sept. 5th. 1887 at Kenley in Surrey and died in France on Nov. 29th. 1917 of wounds received at the battle of Cambrai the night of Nov. 27th.

He loved Learning and Art well, but men and horses better. Himself a brilliant scholar, he held Brilliancy in small esteem ; he valued deeds above words, and prized honesty before all things.

Had he lived longer, some of these poems, revised and re-polished, might have appeared one day in a volume under both our names. Now that he is gone, I dedicate them, as they were left, to the memory of the dearest and bravest brother that a man was ever loved by—animae dimidium meae.

P. S. W.

93

92–3 *Title page and Dedication, by Philip Woolf, of* Poems *by C. N. Sidney Woolf*

private distribution an unknown number of what is surely the rarest of all Hogarth Press publications: a slender white pamphlet, about $5\frac{1}{2}$ by $4\frac{1}{2}$ inches, *Poems by C. N. Sidney Woolf, late 20th Hussars (Spec. Res.) Fellow of Trinity College, Cambridge,* with a dedication by Philip to 'the memory of the dearest and bravest brother that a man was ever loved by —animae dimidium meae'.

At the end of 1918 it would have been difficult to predict much of a future for The Hogarth Press. True, it had made a small paper profit in each of its first two years, but this had involved the expenditure of hundreds of hours of unpaid work for an aggregate output of something less than 400 copies of the three volumes published. This extraordinary drain on the time of Leonard and Virginia proved to be a major problem for nearly thirty years, and led to various proposals for lessening the burden, even to the extent of entirely discontinuing the Press. In 1919 it led to nothing more than a modest change in direction. Leonard and Virginia had agreed to publish a book of poems by a newly made friend —the young American expatriate, T. S. Eliot—who had recently given up schoolmastering and taken a job at Lloyds Bank in London. 'Mr. Eliot', wrote Virginia in a letter to her friend Violet Dickinson, 'is an American of the highest culture, so that his writing is almost unintelligible.' The Hogarth Press was also planning to print *Kew Gardens*, a story written by Virginia. As a third project they took on the publication of *The Critic in Judgment*, a poem by John Middleton Murry. 'Middleton Murry edits the *Athenaeum* and is also very obscure,' explained Virginia. While Virginia respected Murry and wished for his good opinion (both she and Leonard were contributors to the *Athenaeum*), neither she nor Leonard liked Murry—few people did. He was described by an English critic as 'the best-hated man of letters in the country'. The Woolfs did like Katherine Mansfield, who had married Murry in 1918, and it is possible that while they were willing to publish *The Critic in Judgment*, they were not willing to expend the effort needed to set type for it. Whatever the reason, Murry's book was farmed out to a local printer in Richmond, their first venture into commercial production.

All three of the books mentioned: Virginia's *Kew Gardens*, Eliot's *Poems* and Murry's *The Critic in Judgment*, were scheduled for publication on the same date—May 12, 1919. They were, apparently, jointly offered to potential purchasers early in May, and at the same time a more elaborate subscription programme was announced. This provided for two types of subscribers who would make deposits in advance of publication: Deposit 'A' subscribers were to receive each book as issued, while Deposit 'B' subscribers were to receive such books as they should select from the publishers' prospectus. Deposits and orders for the three books began coming in on May 6.* Virginia began to feel the usual pre-publication jitters: 'Murry and Eliot ordered, and not me' based, presumably, on the fact that a Mr Arthur L. Dakyns of Upper Wimpole Street, who had been the first person to subscribe for Publication No. 1, ordered a copy of Eliot's poems and those of Murry but not a copy of *Kew Gardens*, and the same was done by Mr John W. Haines of Hucclecote, near Gloucester.

By May 27, when Leonard and Virginia left Richmond for a week's holiday in Sussex, 42 copies of *Kew Gardens* had been sold. Fable has it —possibly as a result of Virginia's tendency to make a good story better —that at this point *Kew Gardens* was running a poor third among the current Hogarth Press offerings and Virginia was upset by her relatively weak showing. The fact, as recorded in Leonard's account book, was that Virginia's book was doing somewhat better than the other two. At the same date, Eliot's sales were 33 and Murry's 27. But that is only by way of background. The drama occurred on June 3 when Leonard and Virginia returned to Richmond and, on opening the door of Hogarth

---

* Most of the deposits were £1; some, Lady Ottoline Morrell's included, were as low as 10 shillings; the highest deposit received during the several years the plan was operative was £5. Among the £5 subscribers were H. G. Wells, Rebecca West and Vita Sackville-West.

House, found 'the hall table stacked, littered, with orders for *Kew Gardens*'. The *Times Literary Supplement* for May 29, in a half-column review, had described the book as 'a thing of original and therefore strange beauty'. Virginia wrote in her diary ' ... as much praise was allowed me as I like to claim. And 10 days ago I was stoically facing complete failure!' The Woolfs, so excited they could hardly eat dinner, quarrelled, then quickly made up and began the work necessary to fill the orders they had received: 'cutting covers, printing labels, glueing backs, and finally dispatching'. The orders more than exhausted the original supply of 170 copies printed by the Press. Leonard immediately ordered 500 copies from a commercial printer. He saw also the expanded opportunity for the sale of Virginia's earlier writing and decided to reprint *The Mark on the Wall*, her story in Publication No. 1. He ordered 1,000 copies of this pamphlet from a second commercial printer. Thus almost overnight a pastime had become a business. Leonard must have felt so; he ordered a brass name-plate for the door at a cost of 10*s.* 6*d.*

All three of the books were successful ventures. The stock of Eliot's *Poems* (slightly more than 225 were printed) was exhausted in 1920. The second edition of *Kew Gardens* went out of print in 1921. Murry's *The Critic in Judgment* (an edition of 200 copies) was completely sold out by the following year.

The usual payment to authors during these early years of the Press was 25 per cent of the profits. This had been the arrangement with Katherine Mansfield, and it was applied unchanged to Eliot and Murry. Following the precedent of their first publication, Virginia took nothing (except as a partner in The Hogarth Press) for her authorship of *Kew Gardens*. Thus the cost of producing and distributing these books, the payments to the authors, and the profit to the Press were:

	Kew Gardens (first and second editions)			Eliot's *Poems*			*Critic in Judgment*		
	£	*s.*	*d.*	£	*s.*	*d.*	£	*s.*	*d.*
Cost	28	1	8	6	1	10	11	7	7
Payment to author	—			3	2	6	1	13	0
Net profit to Press	14	10	0	9	6	10	5	1	2

Not much for either author or publisher, even by 1919 standards: in that year Virginia received £153 for the 42 reviews she contributed to the *Times Literary Supplement* and *The Athenaeum*—an average of nearly £4 per review.

The three initial ventures into commercial printing which had occurred in 1919 took a more positive turn in the following year with the publication of *Reminiscences of Leo Nicolayevitch Tolstoi* by Maxim Gorky. The book was brought to the Woolfs by a Russian-Jewish refugee, Samuel Solomonavitch Koteliansky, known to everyone inside and outside of Bloomsbury as 'Kot'. Kot had come to England in 1911, had met D. H. Lawrence on a walking tour of the Lake District in 1914, was introduced by Lawrence to Katherine Mansfield and Middleton Murry and by them, probably, to Leonard and Virginia Woolf. According to Katherine Mansfield, Kot had organised an unsuccessful revolution against the Tsar in Kiev: 'On the day appointed for the rising, no one turned up at the meeting-place except Kot; he was so shattered that he started walking, and never stopped till he got to the Tottenham Court Road.'

When Kot approached the Woolfs in 1919 he had recently received a copy of the *Reminiscences* from Gorky, with the right to translate it into English. Kot suggested that he and Leonard jointly should do the translation and that The Hogarth Press should publish it. 'Our actual procedure in translating', Leonard explained, 'was that Kot did the first draft in handwriting, with generous spaces between the lines.' Leonard then turned this 'extremely queer version'—with its phrases such as 'she wore a haggish look'—into English. The book was at least as long as *Prelude* and the Woolfs never again attempted to hand-set anything of that length. Instead, 1,000 copies were ordered from the printer who had produced the second edition of *Kew Gardens*. Gorky's *Reminiscences* was published in July 1920 and did well, selling at a steady rate throughout the rest of the year, and going out of print early in 1921 when a second edition was ordered. The *London Mercury* bought the serial rights in part of the book for £15, and the American rights were sold for £90. Kot received one-half of these payments plus 25 per cent of the total profits; in all some £78 up to the end of April 1924. During the same period profits to the Press from this book, before charging overheads, amounted to a little over £122, considerably more than the aggregate earnings of all previous publications. Six more volumes of Koteliansky translations from the Russian, including works by Tchekhov, Tolstoi and Dostoevsky, followed in the next three years. They were commercially printed and, like the first effort, were surprisingly profitable. Virginia collaborated with Kot in three of these volumes and Leonard in two. In the case of the sixth, a book of short stories by Ivan Bunin, one story was translated by Kot, working with D. H. Lawrence, while the other three were the work of Kot and Leonard. Unfortunately, when they were printed Lawrence's name was accidentally omitted from the

NOTE

The first story in this book, "The Gentleman from San Francisco", is translated by D. H. Lawrence and S. S. Koteliansky. Owing to a mistake Mr. Lawrence's name was omitted from the title-page. The three other stories are translated by Mr. Koteliansky and Mr. Woolf.

THE GENTLEMAN FROM SAN FRANCISCO

AND OTHER STORIES

BY

I. A. BUNIN

TRANSLATED FROM THE RUSSIAN BY

S. S. KOTELIANSKY AND LEONARD WOOLF

PUBLISHED BY LEONARD & VIRGINIA WOOLF AT THE HOGARTH PRESS, PARADISE ROAD, RICHMOND

1922

94 *Title page and Erratum Slip for* The Gentleman from San Francisco

title page. Leonard and Kot were given credit for all the translations in the volume, so that an erratum slip became necessary.

While The Hogarth Press was successfully finding its way into the commercial field with these Russian translations, it was contemporaneously developing an enviable reputation as the publisher of unrecognised and unconventional talent. In 1922 it had published Virginia's *Jacob's Room* and in the following year Eliot's *The Waste Land*, books that have become landmarks of twentieth-century literature. From all sides manuscripts poured into Hogarth House. The Press which had offered one book to the public in 1917, and three in 1919, offered 40 new titles in 1927. This volume of activity inevitably involved substantial modification in the original way of doing business. A larger Minerva platen press—second-hand and worked by a treadle—was purchased in November 1921, on which the Woolfs were able to do improved work. 'Quite professional' was the verdict years later of an expert printer after examining the early work of Leonard and Virginia. But even with the new equipment other demands on the time of the two owners meant that the number of books that were hand-set and hand-printed by them became fewer and fewer, finally ceasing entirely in 1932 after a total of 34 had been produced in this laborious manner. Growth also required that more space be set aside for The Hogarth Press, and this was provided in the basement of the Bloomsbury houses occupied by the Woolfs after 1924. Finally, outside help had to be employed, and one after another the individuals chosen to fill this need moved in and out of the little establishment: Ralph Partridge (1920–3); Marjorie Joad (1923–5); G. W. Rylands (July–December 1924); Angus Davidson (1924–7); Bernadette Murphy (February–July 1925); Mrs Cartwright (1925–30); Richard Kennedy (1929–31); John Lehmann (1931–2) and, for a second time and then as a partner (1938–46).

There were a number of reasons for this procession. First, the matter of pay. Ralph Partridge received £100 a year plus 50 per cent of profits, and for the two-and-a-half years he was with the Press his share came to £41 12s. 4d. Richard Kennedy was taken on at £1 a week. But the money paid was probably the least of the problems. Leonard knew that expenses had to be tightly controlled and risks carefully limited so that the little business would not follow the course toward failure taken by so many well-intentioned artistic enterprises. The Hogarth Press accepted books that were expected to lose money, but only after Leonard had made a dryly realistic computation of what the maximum loss could be and determined that it could be absorbed by the profits from other ventures. Leonard was regarded as a romantic at Cambridge, but there was nothing romantic about his book-keeping. While in the Ceylon Civil Service

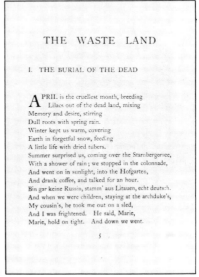

95-6 *Cover and opening page of* The Waste Land

he had evolved a system for recording his personal expenses which he applied without modification to his publishing business. This system eventually caused problems with the Inspector of Taxes, because it was based wholly on cash received and expended, and hence took no account of stock on hand at the beginning and end of the period. But like every business-like book-keeping system, Leonard's required accounting for every halfpenny spent, and the type of employee interested in the aesthetic side of publishing tended to think that the halfpennies were unimportant. Further, because of his conviction that risks must be carefully limited, Leonard was not prepared to abdicate the right to select the books to be published. He knew well enough what had happened to Walter Scott's and Mark Twain's ventures into publishing. Finally, he was not only a demanding task-master, but was inclined to doubt both the facts and the judgment of others, even on matters of minor importance, yielding only to the most incontrovertible evidence. Put more crudely, he was opinionated, he was stubborn, and he enjoyed argument. That he was usually right (and enjoyed being proved right) did not ease the problem of working in peace and harmony with others. In controversy with his subordinates he was capable of working himself into a rage (the strain of living with Virginia may have played some part in this) which did not endear him to the objects of the rage. On one occasion, anxious to prove that Angus Davidson was late, he insisted they go out and check their watches, which varied by two minutes, against the huge clock that hung over the door of Pitman's School in Russell Square. The controversies between John Lehmann and Leonard assumed Homeric proportions.

Virginia's role in the founding of The Hogarth Press has often been questioned. Was not the Press intended as a therapeutic diversion for her? Leonard, in later years, denied that this was the case. Yet we know that the Press was first thought of in 1915, in the midst of the longest period of depression experienced by Virginia, and that when she discontinued type-setting in 1932 she was in relatively good health. And Virginia had no hesitation in acknowledging her debt to the Press: 'I'm the only woman in England free to write what I like. The others must be thinking of series and editions.' But she gave much too, playing a vital part in the operation of the Press from the time of its establishment. She not only set most of the type for an average of two books a year during the period 1917 to 1932, but she also stitched bindings, pasted labels, filled orders and wrapped parcels. She (and Leonard too) learned enough Russian to be able to assist Kot in the translations published by the Press from 1920 to 1923. Virginia got on well with the long succession of male employees who clashed so regularly with Leonard. She was, indeed, one of the reasons that several of them came to the Press. But possibly her most important function was that of attracting new authors and critically reviewing the manuscripts they submitted: 'I read and read and finished I daresay 3 foot thick of MS. read carefully too; much of it on the border, and so needing thought', she noted in 1929. Even after she sold her half interest to John Lehmann in 1938 she continued to advise the Press on literary matters. Some of the most important series of books published by the Press were inaugurated during the period of her more active participation; as for example the 35 volumes of the series called Hogarth Essays, written by people like E. M. Forster, T. S. Eliot, Robert Graves, Edith Sitwell; and the 16 volumes making up the Hogarth Lectures on Literature, whose authors included Rose Macaulay, Harold Nicolson, Edwin Muir and F. L. Lucas. Thus the artistic success of The Hogarth Press owes much to Virginia. Yet full credit must be given to Leonard not only for the business decisions but also for the attraction of many of the authors, particularly those writing about politics and economics. If it had not been for him, the Press could not have lasted very long. It was, in every sense of the term, a joint endeavour dependent on two people of quite remarkable talents. Few husband and wife pairs could have done what the Woolfs were able to accomplish.

There were some negative aspects of the story. One of the consequences of the tight hold that Leonard maintained over the selection of books was that they turned down some that should have been published. Leonard rejected Ivy Compton-Burnett's *Brothers and Sisters*; he also, according to John Lehmann, effectively prevented the acceptance of some early works of Saul Bellow, Sartre and Auden. But the question was not simply whether these works were of high quality. It was whether the Press, which had been operating profitably as a small enterprise, could take on the expansion proposed by Lehmann without incurring losses—losses too heavy for the Press to survive. The issue was not of Lehmann's competence as a judge of literature, which was unquestionably of the highest order, but of his competence as a judge of literature that could be sold profitably in the 1940s. Unfortunately, this issue of substance became confused as the two 'prickly characters', to use Leonard's words, began exchanging unpleasantly worded notes. Lehmann saw only one solution: to dissolve the partnership. The partnership agreement provided that if one partner notified the other of his decision to terminate the partnership, the partner receiving the notice had the option of buying out the partner who gave notice. Lehmann gave notice in January 1946. Woolf promptly advised Lehmann that he would exercise his option to buy Lehmann's shares, and arranged through Ian Parsons for Chatto & Windus to acquire two-thirds of the Press's equity. As a consequence, Lehmann received back all his original capital plus a profit of more than 100 per cent on the money he and his family had invested in the Press. Indeed this seems to have been one of the most profitable ventures in Lehmann's long career as a publisher, and was followed by the bitter experiences described at length in his autobiography, in the years after he left The Hogarth Press.

The allegation that Leonard turned down some books is, in any event, hardly damaging criticism, since there has never been a publisher who has not turned down some books that, in retrospect, he should have accepted. However, the Woolfs did not, as has sometimes been suggested, turn down Joyce's *Ulysses*. Parts of the book (it was not yet finished) were brought to them by T. S. Eliot's employer on the magazine *Egoist*, Miss Harriet Weaver: 'a very mild blue eyed advanced spinster' who had 'the table manners ... of a well bred hen'. Virginia read the manuscript and although she did not find it completely to her taste, she was 'amused, stimulated, charmed, interested' and thought it displayed 'Genius ... but of the inferior water'. Leonard tried to find a printer for it, which in itself was an act of courage in 1918, but could find no one who would dare to undertake it.

Regardless of what the Woolfs might have done but did not do, what they *did* do was a success. From the time The Hogarth Press was founded in 1917 until Virginia's death in 1941 (and beyond), it operated profitably. During this period, The Hogarth Press published more than 400 books which, with rare exceptions, were works of unusual distinction. The list of authors of this youthful venture, some of whom have already been mentioned, cannot be matched by any large established publishing firm over any equal period. In the first four years of its existence The Hogarth Press published the works of four individuals whose names cannot be omitted from any history of writing in the twentieth century: Virginia Woolf, T. S. Eliot, Katherine Mansfield and E. M. Forster. Others who were published under the Hogarth imprint include Robert Graves, Christopher Isherwood, Rose Macaulay, Harold Nicolson, William Plomer, Herbert Read, Edith Sitwell, Gertrude Stein, V. Sackville-West, Stephen Spender, Hugh Walpole, H. G. Wells, Rebecca West and the last two Poets Laureate: C. Day Lewis and John Betjeman. But that hardly tells the full story. The Hogarth Press were the first publishers in England of three American poets: John Crowe Ransom, Robinson Jeffers and Edward Arlington Robinson. They published the

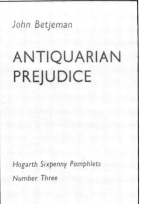

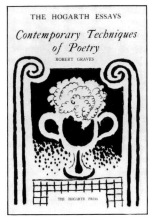

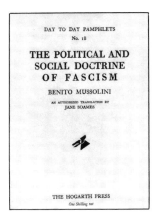

97 *Pages and covers of nine Hogarth Press publications*

works of continental authors not previously printed in English: for example, the poetry of Rainer Maria Rilke and the novels of Italo Svevo, a protégé of James Joyce. In addition, the Press published writings on disarmament by Philip Noel-Baker, who later won the Nobel Prize for his work on this subject; writings on economics by John Maynard Keynes; and writings on psychology by Sigmund Freud.

The announcement issued by The Hogarth Press on its fifth anniversary stated that 'our first publication *Two Stories* by Leonard and Virginia Woolf, originally published at one shilling and sixpence, now fetches twenty-five shillings in the second-hand bookshops'. This was in 1922. On December 16, 1974 a copy of the same publication was sold in London at Sotheby's for £380. T. S. Eliot's *Poems*, published by the Press at two shillings and sixpence, has not appeared at public auction for a number of years, but a copy has recently been offered by an American bookseller for 650 dollars.

Leonard kept a few mint copies of these early books in the old steamer trunk which he had taken with him to Ceylon in 1904; it still bears the original P&O labels and the legend 'not needed on voyage'. While Leonard thought collectors of first editions were highly irrational, he knew the value of what he had set aside. Not long before his death he told a visitor, pointing to the trunk in Virginia's room: 'These are the books the collectors will be after.' He was right.

[8]

CAREERS: YEARS OF
TRIUMPH

98 *Detail of tiled fireplace by Vanessa Bell at Monks House, showing the Lighthouse*

1923–9

In 1923, a year in which The Hogarth Press had published fourteen books, Leonard had taken a 'paid job' on a part-time basis. The circumstances were these: Maynard Keynes, with some associates, acquired control of the *Nation*, a weekly periodical which was a competitor of the *New Statesman*. Leonard was offered the job of Literary Editor, and accepted it on the understanding that he would not spend more than two-and-a-half days a week at the office and would be allowed to undertake freelance work for other journals as well as his work at the Press.

'He is a masterly man,' wrote Virginia at the time. 'In 2 days he does what a thoroughly good editor spreads over a week.' As Literary Editor he gave his reviewers a free hand, refusing to interfere with signed contributions 'except in extreme cases (or where libel or indecency makes it dangerous for the paper)'. He liked reviews in which the book being reviewed was given a 'slating', adding that 'the more good-humoured and even tempered and non-rude the slater is, the most effective I believe the slating to be'. These standards were completely acceptable to the poet Richard Aldington, a naturally quarrelsome man, who regularly reviewed for Leonard. 'I write for you', he said in a letter dated March 4, 1926, 'with more ease and zest than for any other editor I ever worked for ... You give all the liberty one could reasonably ask, and yet at the same time I always feel perfectly confident you wouldn't allow me to print anything really foolish or unwise.' Raymond Mortimer, another of his reviewers during this period, reported that 'Leonard as my boss on the *Nation* always proved considerate'.

The *Nation* paid Leonard £500 a year, and with these regular earnings the Woolfs were finally able to meet their living expenses out of current income. Because of the increasing success of Virginia's books over the next few years, the income from the *Nation* became of diminishing importance and Leonard was thus able to reduce the quantity of his work for it (with a corresponding reduction in his salary) in 1924, and again in 1926. He gave the job up entirely in 1930. During the time Leonard was Literary Editor he published few books;* but it was one of Virginia's most prolific periods.

In 1925 *Mrs Dalloway* was published. It tells two parallel stories that occur in the same 24 hours, stories connected by thin ties of coincidence: a day in the life of Clarissa Dalloway, which culminates in a party at her Westminster home, and the last day in the life of Septimus Smith, who dies after throwing himself out of a window. In *Mrs Dalloway*, as in Virginia's other novels, most of the characters are derived from people she knew. Many of Clarissa Dalloway's characteristics ('the perfect hostess') are taken from Virginia's childhood friend, Kitty Maxse, who died in 1922 after a fall which Virginia believed was suicide. Much of Virginia's own experience during her madness is told as the experience of Septimus Smith.

People who insist on a 'story' in the novels they read are sometimes disappointed by *Mrs Dalloway*. For *Mrs Dalloway* is devoted to further speculation on the continuing theme What is life? What is love? Vir-

---

* The only full-length book published was a volume of collected essays in 1927.

ginia seems to say that life is almost as many things as there are people; it is largely the vision one creates of it: 'one makes up the better part of life'. And love is an unexplainable experience, only to be described in the most tentative terms.

The sales of *Mrs Dalloway* showed that Virginia's select audience was steadily growing in size. In England and the United States over 8,000 copies were printed in 1925, nearly double the 4,700 copies of *Jacob's Room* printed in its first year. In 1925 Virginia also put together a number of book reviews and essays under the title *The Common Reader*. Max Beerbohm, who found Virginia's novels unreadable because they failed to tell a story in the traditional way ('Your novels beat me—black and blue') rated *The Common Reader* 'above any modern book of criticism'. The favourable reception of these two books in America during the spring of 1925 presumably accounts for one of the most remarkable essays ever written by Virginia: her article on American fiction, published in an American literary review in the summer of the same year. Remarkable, because it so effectively demonstrates Virginia's literary perception and at the same time so completely demolishes any conception of her as nothing but a sickly, introspective aesthete. For she had read Ring Lardner's *You Know Me Al*—a story which few people outside the United States would have bothered to look at and which few people within the United States thought of as anything more than the crude effusions of a funny man—a story about the American game of baseball, written in American slang about American low-brows—and recognised it for what it was: 'the best prose that has come our way'.

The year 1926 was the turning point in Virginia's literary career. With two new books out, and growing public recognition, articles by her were much in demand, particularly in the United States. In 1925 Virginia's income from her writings was £223. In 1926 it was £713. Three years later it had risen to £2,936.* This abrupt jump was due to the success of her next two books: *To the Lighthouse*, published in 1927, and *Orlando* published in 1928.

To the Lighthouse has proved the most popular of all Virginia Woolf's books. It has been translated into thirteen languages, and over half-a-million copies of it have been sold in English language editions alone. Once again the material for it was derived from Virginia's family. Although the reader is presented with a Mr and Mrs Ramsay on holiday with their children and friends at their summer home in Skye, the actual

---

* Simultaneously, the profits of The Hogarth Press, in which Virginia was a 50 per cent partner, increased greatly as a result of the success of her books.

characters are Mr and Mrs Leslie Stephen, and the setting is their summer home at St Ives, Cornwall. The book describes them and their relationship to each other and to those around them. It is unique among literary biographies, for what author has so lovingly, yet so mercilessly and honestly, rendered both the black and the white of his parents? 'He was an adorable man and somehow tremendous,' says Virginia of her father in one of her letters, yet in *To the Lighthouse* he is described with all his wisdom and integrity on the one hand, and all his irritable unreasonableness on the other. That he was adorable to Virginia did not prevent her from seeing him as 'the very figure of a famished wolfhound' —and pictures of Leslie Stephen confirm the appropriateness of the simile. Her mother's goodness and her habit of injecting herself into the affairs of others, are rendered with equal impartiality. Vanessa, on reading the book declared:

... you have given a portrait of mother which is more like her to me than anything I could ever have conceived of as possible. It is almost painful to have her so raised from the dead ... You have given father too I think as clearly ... it seems to me the only thing about him which ever gave a true idea. So you see as far as portrait painting goes you seem to be a supreme artist and it is so shattering to find oneself face to face with those two again that I can hardly consider anything else.

People argued about what the book meant, and the significance of the Lighthouse. Virginia said it meant *nothing*. But meaning or no meaning, readers liked *To the Lighthouse* as they have liked other works— *Kubla Khan* or *Tristram Shandy*—whose 'meaning' it would be impossible to define.

Orlando was completed in the shortest time of any of Virginia's novels. It was written primarily for her amusement and for the amusement of Vita Sackville-West, to whom it was dedicated. *Orlando* is a biography of Vita. Virginia began with these ingredients: Vita herself—a successful poet and novelist; a dark beauty—lover of both men and women— particularly proud of her shapely legs, the loving wife of a distinguished diplomat who was also a homosexual; the mother of his two sons; an aristocrat with a strain of illegitimate gypsy blood who grew up surrounded by wealth, disliked society, loved the country and had a passionate attachment to Knole, the great house in Kent which had been in the possession of her family since 1586. These disparate elements are woven into a fantasy that portrays twenty years of Vita's life from the age of 16 to 36 as though this life had been lived between 1586 and 1928: ' ... a little fiction mixed with fact can be made to transmit personality very effectively', Virginia had written in 1927. Orlando begins the story as a boy and half-way through magically changes into a woman. Many of Virginia's private jokes about Vita's transvestite frolics and homosexual and heterosexual love affairs were not accessible to the ordinary reader until the publication, in 1973, of *Portrait of a Marriage* in which Vita's son, Nigel Nicolson, has quoted liberally from his mother's letters and other private papers.

Orlando reflects Virginia's soaring, imaginative, teasing manner, more than any of her other writing. Her sense of fun runs through the book, and is not limited to jokes about Vita. At one point she inserts a little verse written out as though it were prose: 'Let us go, then, exploring, this summer morning, when all are adoring the plum blossom and the bee.' When writing about the eighteenth-century literary scene she covertly slips in a pun on the name of her friend Sybil Colefax, the London hostess of the 1920s: 'The hostess is our modern Sibyl. She is a witch who lays her guests under a spell.'* And there are witticisms of another character: 'She ... held some caprices which are more common among women than men, as for instance that to travel south is to travel downhill.'

With all this in the book it is no surprise that *Orlando* proved as popular as it did. The first printings in England and America (including a small limited edition) totalled about 12,000 copies, substantially in excess of the whole first year's sales of *To the Lighthouse*. These were immediately sold out and second impressions printed within a month of publication. (The first paperback printings of *Orlando* in England and America, nearly twenty years later, totalled 278,000 copies.)

In 1928 Virginia was asked to speak to the Arts Society of Newnham College Cambridge on 'Women and Fiction'. The paper delivered in October of that year, later expanded into *A Room of One's Own*, was an opening shot in the modern feminist movement. Compare, Virginia suggested, a luncheon at a men's college (presumably Trinity or King's) with a dinner at Newnham. The masculine meal included soles spread with 'a counterpane of the whitest cream ... branded here and there with spots like the spots on the flanks of a doe'; 'partridges, many and various ... with all their retinue of sauces'; 'potatoes, thin as coins'; 'sprouts, foliated as rosebuds but more succulent'; and 'a confection which rose all sugar from the waves'—served while wine-glasses 'flushed yellow and crimson'. In contrast, the women's dinner included beef 'suggesting the rumps of cattle in a muddy market' and custard with prunes 'as stringy as a miser's heart'; a meal washed down with a liberal supply of water. Men

---

* Virginia was probably also having fun with Aunt Annie Ritchie, who had written 'A Discourse on Modern Sibyls'. Lady Ritchie, *From the Porch* (1913).

had the money; they had discouraged women from obtaining the education and experience essential to get money. And if women are going to write fiction or poetry, 'it is necessary to have five hundred a year and a room with a lock on the door'.

By the time *A Room of One's Own* was published in 1929, Virginia had developed an audience large enough to assure the success of any new book. In six months more than 22,000 copies were sold in Britain and the United States.

1930–40

In 1929 Virginia's royalties reached nearly £3,000, and the profits of The Hogarth Press reached £380. Her income alone was almost three times the amount the Woolfs needed for their living expenses. In consequence, as we have seen, Leonard was able to give up his job at the *Nation* entirely. He was then 49 and never again took on any regular full-time employment.

In 1930 the Woolfs began to spend more time in the country. They spent many weekends at Monks House, their home in Sussex, and were there throughout August and September—overall a third of the year. Leonard occupied himself with the business of The Hogarth Press, which he estimated took a quarter of his time, and devoted the rest to writing and several public activities.* The writing included occasional articles for the *Nation* (which became the *New Statesman* after 1931 when the two combined) and for the *Political Quarterly*, which Leonard helped to found in 1930. He was also able to concentrate on a work that had been in his mind for a long time—a text on political philosophy entitled *After the Deluge*. The 'deluge' referred to the First World War. The book, published in 1931 as the first in a series that Leonard thought would require 'a good many volumes', was an attempt to understand the causes of that war. Beginning with the belief that the causes were psychological, Leonard set out to demonstrate this by investigating scientifically certain major events in history. The first volume examined the psychological factors in the French Revolution of 1789, and the development of the concept of democracy.

The reviews were mixed. Russell Sedgwick in *Time and Tide*, although stating that the book was important and one that 'no mentally active citizen ... can afford to neglect', claimed that the treatment lacked

---

* Principally the Labour Party Advisory Committees on which Leonard served as Secretary. During 1930 he attended 27 of such meetings.

psychological background and condemned Leonard's habit of 'dogmatic exaggeration'. The *Times Literary Supplement* contained some compliments but damned the book with the statement that its treatment of the General Strike of 1926 'tails away into cheapness'. Sales were only modest in the first year, but it was reprinted as a Penguin paperback in 1937.

The same year, 1931, saw the publication of *The Waves*, a novel in which Virginia tried to portray the essence of six characters—three men and three women—their lives from childhood to the grave as seen by themselves and each other and their relationship to a seventh character: Percival, drawn from her brother Thoby, who had appeared nine years before in *Jacob's Room*. Although in an adulterated form, several of the principal characters are readily identifiable: Rhoda is Virginia herself, and indeed the novel is largely autobiographical, with the recollections of her childhood at St Ives and brief references to more recent events such as her trip to Spain in 1923, her viewing of an eclipse in 1927. The recurrent imagery of the sea in *The Waves* (and elsewhere) also has autobiographical significance: 'The sea is a miracle' wrote Virginia in 1908, 'more congenial to me than any human being'. Jinny seems derived from Kitty Maxse or perhaps Mary Hutchinson, Clive Bell's friend at that time; Bernard is taken from Desmond MacCarthy; Louis from Leonard; Neville from Lytton Strachey. To those who believe that reality is a description of physical functions *The Waves* must appear unreal—'all about nothing' as Hugh Walpole put it. To those who believe that reality is a function of the mind, *The Waves* is vitally real.* Angus Wilson called it 'one of the three greatest English novels of this century'. The public liked it well enough to justify second impressions, within a month, in both England and the United States.

In 1932 another volume of Virginia's articles and reviews—*The Common Reader: Second Series*—was issued. This was put together while Virginia was thinking about and writing her next two books: *Flush* and *The Years*. *Flush, A Biography*, issued in 1932, was about the adventures in London and Florence of Elizabeth Browning's spaniel. It was based on some facts ('there are very few authorities for the foregoing biography') plus a large quantity of imagination aided by a close association with 'Pinka', a cocker spaniel that Vita had given Virginia. No credit in the book is given to Pinka, who posed for the

---

* ' ... for folks that have any fancy in 'em, such beautiful dreams is the real part o' life ... But to most folks the common things that happens outside 'em is all in all.' Sarah Orne Jewett, *The Country of the Pointed Firs*, The Traveller's Library (1951), p. 229.

frontispiece, or to Leonard who took the picture. *Flush* was enormously successful—for the wrong reasons, Virginia thought—with the largest first edition ever printed of any of her books, and the need for further impressions in the next few months: nearly 50,000 copies in England and the United States.

While Leonard continued to work at what was to be his magnum opus, the successor volumes to *After the Deluge* in which he expressed his long-term view of history, his immediate attention was diverted by the rise of Hitler and Mussolini and the increasing tension in Europe. In 1935 he published *Quack, Quack!* a bitter attack on irrationalism in politics as exemplified by Nazi Germany and Fascist Italy, and in philosophy as revealed in the writings of Spengler, Keyserling, Radhakrishnan and Bergson.

Virginia's next novel, *The Years*, was published in 1937. For over two-thirds of its length it reverted to the straightforward method of telling a story in the accepted tradition of English novels; a method Virginia had not used since *Night and Day*. It related events in the lives of members of the Pargiter family from 1880 to 1918. The final chapter, 'The Present Day', brings together the remnants of the family at a party in Bloomsbury, as Thomas Love Peacock brought his characters together for a weekend in the country. Here again Virginia pursues that elusive question: What is life?

The writing of *The Years* had been difficult for Virginia and the prospect of its publication put her under great strain. She thought it too long and too minute, got 'sick to death of it; and took Leonard's garden scissors and cut out patches and flung them on the bonfire'. It had been six years since the success of *The Waves* and four since *Flush* had been published. Attacks by Wyndham Lewis and others had made it plain that failure at this point would be greeted with glee in certain quarters. Despite the concern felt by Virginia, *The Years* proved her greatest financial success. Over 5,000 copies were sold before publication. The first English edition was for 18,000 copies. In America it became a best-seller and nearly 50,000 copies were sold there in the first year.

The female characters in *The Years* reminded Virginia that she had not said all that could be said on the subject of discrimination when she wrote *A Room of One's Own* in 1929. Also, some things had happened since then to keep the sensitive nerve alive. In 1935, for example, Morgan Forster, a member of the Committee of the London Library, told her that the Committee had decided that women would be impossible as Committee members. A book called *Three Guineas* gradually took shape and was published in 1938. Although many of her close friends (mostly men) thought that it was unnecessarily shrill—it is true that it had none of the good humour of the earlier book—its value as a polemic must be judged by how much it accomplished rather than by how much it was liked. As to that, no measure exists; any conclusion depends on how many other women were inspired by the book to carry on the fight. All we know is that the book has become another landmark in the feminist movement, and that much has occurred in the past forty years to reduce the extent of discrimination against women in education, in the professions, and in government employment: areas that come under particular attack in this book.

Roger Fry had died in 1934 while Virginia was writing *The Years*. Importuned by Fry's sister and some of his friends, Virginia undertook to write his biography. This proved a harrowing experience. Her factual writing had always been in the form of essays; whereas a full biography, with its need to marshall a lifetime of facts, was a formidable physical burden for one who was neither accustomed to working with elaborate files nor to sorting out mountains of miscellaneous information on to index cards. Further, Virginia found herself unable to write fully and frankly about Fry's love-life, and particularly about his relations with her sister Vanessa. Despite these problems, *Roger Fry*, published in 1940, is a thoughtful and perceptive biography by one who knew him well. The description of Fry motoring through Europe with J. P. Morgan and Morgan's mistress is one of the funniest travelogues in literature. To everyone it was not equally funny. Violent transatlantic pressures, including representations through Maynard Keynes and Lord Bicester, a partner in Morgan Grenfell, were exerted to delete this episode from the American edition. The efforts were unsuccessful, but the New York papers gallantly failed to mention the incident in their reviews.

Leonard, in the meanwhile, was addressing himself directly to the growing threat of war. In 1939 he published three books on this subject. In *Barbarians at the Gate** he concluded that the danger to civilisation was not Hitler, Mussolini or the Nazi and Fascist systems—not in the barbarians at the gate—but from forces within the citadel; it was the capitalist systems in France and Britain, and the repression of liberties in Russia. For although Leonard believed that the ultimate aims of Russian communism were a civilisation based upon the western concepts of freedom, nevertheless, and much to his credit, he was one of the first English socialists to condemn the authoritarian dictatorship of Stalin: 'So far as the control and use of power goes, there is no difference

* Published in the United States as *Barbarians Within and Without*.

between the position of Stalin and the group which surrounds him and that of Hitler and Mussolini and the groups surrounding them.' *Barbarians at the Gate* was published in England by the Left Book Club despite the violent objection of John Strachey, one of the three Left Book Club judges, and a confirmed apologist for Stalin's Russia.

The second volume of *After the Deluge* was also published in 1939. Following the first volume by eight years, it examined the Reform Act of 1832 in England and the French Revolution of 1830 — 'the first attempts in the 19th century to translate the ideas and principles of democracy into practice'.

Leonard's play *The Hotel* was the third of his books to appear in 1939. Most of the action takes place in the hall of a hotel. The plot, to quote the dust wrapper, 'turns on the manoeuvres of Nazi and Communist agents to obtain possession of a consignment of arms' for shipment to Spain. The play ends after the senseless death of the innocent Christopher (Christian), son of the chambermaid, Mary, and Vajoff, proprietor of the Grand Hotel de l'Univers et du Commerce. *The Hotel* was a drama with a message expressed in irony and symbolism — a difficult combination. Less than 1,000 copies were sold and repeated efforts to secure a performance were unsuccessful.

In the following year Leonard reverted to a more familiar theme with the publication of *The War for Peace* — a plea for an international system, based on law, compromise and co-operation, to prevent war. Why had the League of Nations failed? What elements were necessary to create a new system that would work? These were the questions to which *The War for Peace* was addressed.

Virginia's last novel, *Between the Acts*, was conceived before war broke out but was written mostly after Germany invaded Poland in August 1939. It reflects her concern with the civilisation that was threatened by the war, and with the individuals who were being called on to save that civilisation. *Between the Acts*, like *Mrs Dalloway*, is limited to a period of 24 hours. The action all takes place at an old English house, Pointz Hall, which had been the home of the present occupants, the Olivers, for 'only something over a hundred and twenty years'. The high point of the day is the annual village pageant, a review of the history of England ending in a scene in which the audience is confronted by a view of themselves through looking glasses held before them by the assembled cast. They are asked how civilisation is to be built by 'orts, scraps, and fragments like ourselves'? Nearly every major character in the book is lonely, a recurring theme in Virginia's novels. Much of the aridity of *Between the Acts* is reminiscent of T. S. Eliot's

The Waste Land and, not surprisingly, Eliot thought it her best novel. At the time of Virginia's death in March 1941 *Between the Acts* had been completed but not finally revised for the printer.

Anyone who reads the critical reviews of *Between the Acts* will notice the wide diversity of opinion on the meaning of Virginia's last contribution to English literature. Critics seem to be driven by the need to find an easy answer; to sum up the meaning in some simple sentence on which, apparently, no two can agree. But surely Virginia herself would have done that if she had thought it could be done; she was not setting a riddle to which she held the answer. What then, was she doing? Her essay 'The Russian Point of View' suggests a reply. Writing of Tchekhov, she said:

These stories are inconclusive, we say, and proceed to frame a criticism based upon the assumption that stories ought to conclude in a way that we recognise. In so doing, we raise the question of our own fitness as readers.

Returning to the same subject, she continued:

Nothing is solved, we feel; nothing is rightly held together. On the other hand, the method which at first seemed so casual, inconclusive, and occupied with trifles, now appears the result of an exquisitely original and fastidious taste, choosing boldly, arranging infallibly, and controlled by an honesty for which we can find no match save among the Russians themselves.... In consequence, as we read these little stories about nothing at all, the horizon widens; the soul gains an astonishing sense of freedom.

Is it not likely that by showing us our own inadequacies with unflinching honesty, by exposing 'affectation, pose and insincerity', giving us her 'vision' in *Between the Acts*, Virginia intended no more than to widen our horizon and to give us a new sense of freedom?

99 *Vanessa, with her sons Julian and Quentin, and Roger Fry*

[9]

OLD FRIENDS
AND NEW

100 *Vanessa, Clive Bell and Duncan Grant*

Bloomsbury was a casualty of the First World War. It 'vanished like the morning mist' to use Virginia's words. 'It is so long since I have seen Lytton', she wrote on April 17, 1919, 'that I take my impression of him too much from his writing'; she was referring to one of his recent articles which she did not like. In 1920 an effort was made to recapture some of the past. Leonard and Virginia joined with eleven old friends to form the Memoir Club. The others were Clive and Vanessa Bell, Desmond and Molly MacCarthy, Lytton Strachey, Roger Fry, Morgan

Forster, Maynard Keynes, Duncan Grant, Saxon Sydney-Turner and Sydney Waterlow. These individuals, according to Leonard, were 'identical with the original thirteen members of old Bloomsbury'.*

When the Memoir Club was founded, sixteen years had elapsed since Virginia and Vanessa had moved to Gordon Square with their two brothers. In that period much had happened to account for a change in relationships. Most of the members of the group were now in their late thirties or early forties; inevitably they had gone their several ways and become immersed in their separate careers. Four of them—Clive Bell, Lytton Strachey, Morgan Forster and Maynard Keynes—had written books which were outstandingly successful and which won them considerable reputations in their respective fields of art criticism, biography, fiction and economics.

There were other changes as well. The two Stephen brothers had been lost to Bloomsbury—Thoby by death and Adrian by marriage, for in 1915 Adrian had married Karin Costelloe, whom Virginia and Vanessa found somewhat unsympathetic. Vanessa and Clive had lived together as man and wife for a few years after their marriage, and then had amicably gone their separate ways. For a short period Vanessa and Roger Fry had been lovers (1911–14), then Duncan Grant took Roger's place. Duncan in his younger days had been Maynard's lover ('that Mr. Grant', said Maud, house-maid at Fitzroy Square in 1913, 'gets in everywhere'), but now, while Duncan was living with Vanessa, Maynard had fallen in love with the Russian prima ballerina Lydia Lopokova, whom he married in 1925. At such a club, one can see infinite opportunities for topics of discussion devoted to 'memoirs'.

But Leonard's personal diary, in which he recorded the people he had seen every day, makes it plain that the Memoir Club had, at most, only a brief success in resurrecting old Bloomsbury, which became a diminishing element in the Woolfs' lives as the years went on. In 1913 Leonard saw the others in the group (exclusive of Vanessa's household, which included Clive and Duncan) about once a month. His 1938 diary shows that he was seeing the others, on average, only about twice a year. The Memoir Club itself gradually dwindled. Sydney Waterlow dropped out soon after it was formed. David Garnett was added, and later the three children of Vanessa Bell were invited to join, but the numerous later replacements tended to derive less and less from old Bloomsbury,

---

* *Downhill All the Way* (1967) p. 114. When Leonard wrote this he had apparently forgotten that in the prior volume of his autobiography, *Beginning Again* (1964) p.22, the list he gave of the original thirteen members of old Bloomsbury included Adrian Stephen but not Sydney Waterlow.

and the club itself expired in the late 1950s. Several decades before that, old Bloomsbury had become a ghost.* Virginia's diary entry for September 2, 1930, ten years after the Memoir Club was founded reads: 'I seldom see Lytton ... Morgan I keep up with in our chronically spasmodic way ... Adrian I never see. I keep constant with Maynard. I never see Saxon.'

There is always the temptation to think of these interesting people as a group, as they have been dealt with here, but there has rarely been a group of this size in which there were wider disparities in personality and points of view. The common bonds were frankness, the enjoyment of conversation, a respect for intelligence and reason, a belief in personal freedom, long association and a certain amount of affection. Although an outsider might find evidence of group solidarity, particularly on the art side, internally it was never a mutual admiration society. Saxon thought that their only distinctive characteristic was that 'we were all rather nice'. But they did not always speak of each other as equally nice. They freely

---

* The table lists the number of times the names of the other eleven members of the Memoir Club (and Adrian Stephen) appear in Leonard's diary in 1913 — the last year before the war — compared with 1919 — the first year after the war — and four later dates. Since Leonard's diary rarely states who was in attendance at the Memoir Club meetings (which were held about twice a year) the figures are principally for meetings that took place outside the club:

	L&V living in London	L&V living in Richmond		L&V living in London		
	1913	1919	1923	1928	1933	1938
Vanessa	43	9	13	36	42	39
Clive	28	5	17	23	6	9
Duncan	14	6	5	8	4	10
Desmond	15	1	5	7	8	2
Molly	6	1	0	1	2	2
Roger	15	3	8	14	5	d.
Sydney	19	1	0	0	0	0
Maynard	5	4	8	9	9	9
Lytton	20	5	5	7	d.	d.
Morgan	6	7	8	6	5	4
Saxon	20	4	5	3	1	0
Adrian	32	4	2	2	1	2
Total	223	50	76	116	83	77
Excluding Vanessa, Clive and Duncan	138	30	41	49	31	19

d. = deceased

criticised each other and joked about each other in much the way members of an outspoken family do. Maynard Keynes was a genius and amusing and he could be kindly; but he was a person who, though often fun to be with, had certain abrasive characteristics to those who knew him well. When Leonard was in Ceylon he had no kind thoughts about Maynard: 'who, if he has the face of a pig', wrote Leonard to Lytton (presumably in reply to what Lytton had said in a letter to him) 'has the soul of a goat'. 'I detest Keynes, don't you? ... I see he is fundamentally evil if ever anyone was', was another message Leonard sent Lytton from Ceylon. Virginia regarded Maynard's kindness as superficial. In 1923 Morgan Forster stated that Keynes was 'a curious mixture of benevolence and school-boy selfishness ... I should work under him if I needed money and was certain to get it—not otherwise.' Outsiders were even harsher in their judgments. Kingsley Martin, who as editor of the *New Statesman* worked for Maynard (a director and major shareholder of the periodical) wrote in 1945: 'I have always liked Maynard and stood up for him to other people who accuse him of being arrogant, rude and all the rest of it ... But I am never again going to subject myself to his insults ... I understand now why people hate Maynard so much.' Continuing, he quoted a Cambridge don who had said that 'the dominant characteristic of Maynard was cruelty'.*

Virginia found Roger Fry stimulating, but thought 'his attempts to keep with the young' (Roger was sixteen years older than Virginia) 'rather pathetic'. Lytton did not like Roger, calling him 'a most shifty and wormy character'. Leonard wrote that '90% of him was ... gentleness and scrupulousness, but there was ... a streak—say 10%—completely contradictory ... He had this curious ruthless streak.' Leonard saw a parallel flaw in Lytton who 'could be the most entrancing companion, but when in the mood, intolerant and intolerable' and 'would display, on occasions, an almost contemptuous, if not unscrupulous, disregard of accuracy in detail'.

The ineffectual Saxon had been viewed by his friends with 'amused affection' almost from the start. 'He upset the ink at breakfast', wrote Virginia in 1909, 'and tried to clean his chair with the end of a handkerchief dipped in milk ... Then he cleaned a pair of scissors on a piece of bread.' But in his later years (he lived until 1962) he became something of a bore and a burden to others. In 1942 Sydney Waterlow, back from

---

* Unfortunately, Maynard's 'official' biography, *The Life of John Maynard Keynes* by Roy Harrod (1951), makes little attempt to evaluate this side of his character. The recent *Essays on John Maynard Keynes* (1975) edited by his nephew Milo Keynes, is also disappointing in this respect although it is franker about his early homosexual activities.

101 *Roger Fry with Vanessa Bell*
102 *Roger Fry in the upstairs sitting room, Monks House*
103 *Duncan Grant*
104 *Duncan Grant with Barbara Bagenal at Charleston in 1917, wearing the costumes he had designed for 'Pelléas et Mélisande'. Courtesy Barbara Bagenal*

service abroad, wrote that visits from Saxon 'actually devastate me'. After Saxon retired, he sat in his rooms in Percy Street gambling away his small pension on horses and the stock market. On at least one occasion Vanessa stood the cost of his groceries so that he could live until his next pension cheque was due.

Desmond was charming, but his unpunctuality 'amounted almost to genius'. Because of it he was never able to produce the great book expected of him by his friends. This lack of firmness was upsetting to Virginia. 'Desmond has an abnormal power for depressing me', she wrote in her diary on June 1, 1925. 'He takes the edge off life in some extraordinary way. I love him; but his balance and goodness and humour, all heavenly in themselves, somehow diminish lustre.'

Leonard was renowned for his stubbornness and eccentricity; he and Vanessa did not always hit it off well, and Virginia tended to side with Leonard. Virginia was regarded as a bad security risk, since anything she was told was likely to be retold, usually with Byzantine ornamentation. Morgan Forster and Leonard had an extremely close relationship, but Virginia, although greatly valuing Forster's criticism, never felt completely comfortable with him, nor he with her. Clive Bell came in for more than his fair share of abuse. He had been knowledgeable about horses and guns when he went up to Cambridge and hence was thought of as an outsider, a likeable character but rather shallow. 'He has a simple rather sunny nature, a bright serviceable little mind,' wrote Leonard about his brother-in-law. Everyone agreed he talked too loudly. Roger Fry claimed Clive had stolen various ideas on art from him. Virginia alternately liked Clive and was exasperated with him, called him a 'cockatoo' and a 'little hop o' my thumb' (he was almost two inches shorter than Virginia's 5 ft 10 in.), said that he reminded her of a cherub — 'all bottom and a little flaxen wig'.

The decline of old Bloomsbury as a factor in the lives of Leonard and Virginia was offset by new relationships. Katherine Mansfield appeared late in 1916 or early in 1917, and she and Virginia were intrigued with each other. Like a puppy seeing itself for the first time in a mirror, neither had previously known a woman whose life was devoted wholly to writing. Virginia found that Katherine was equally possessed by demons of the pen: 'No one felt more seriously the importance of writing than she did.' And Katherine had a similar reaction: 'Pray consider', said Katherine in a letter to Virginia, 'how rare it is to find some one with the same passion for writing that you have, who desires to be scrupulously truthful with you — and to give you the freedom of the city without any reserves at all.' Yet there was something in their natures

05

106

107

105 *E. M. Forster*
106 *Saxon Sydney-Turner with Judith Bagenal c. 1920*
107 *Desmond and Molly MacCarthy*

108 *Virginia with Lytton Strachey in the garden at Ottoline Morrell's house in Gower Street*

109 *Virginia with Adrian and Karin Stephen*

that prevented them from forming a solid friendship. Katherine may have been put off by Virginia's proper background, or Virginia may have been upset by the self-destructiveness of Katherine's life and her vagabond ways. Perhaps the unpleasant Middleton Murry, Katherine's lover and later her husband, was an obstacle. Virginia wrote seventeen articles for his magazine the *Athenaeum* in 1919 and 1920, but almost from the first found him 'mud-coloured and mute'. Later, when she knew him better, she saw him as 'a posturing Byronic little man; pale; penetrating; with bad teeth; histrionic; an egoist; not, I think, very honest ...' Virginia's friendship was cut short when Katherine left for Italy in 1920, after which they never saw each other again. Katherine wrote that she was 'a bit "haunted"' by Virginia, remembering her, with her head a little on one side, smiling as though she 'knew some enchanting secret'. For Virginia, Katherine was an experience she never forgot. Twenty years after they parted she still recalled incidents in their conversations.

T. S. Eliot entered the scene in 1918 when he visited Hogarth House armed with some of his poems, which he read aloud to Leonard and Virginia. Eliot interested Virginia as a person, as a poet and as a literary critic. Unlike Katherine Mansfield he was inhibited and appeared cold. He told a friend that he had never shaved in front of his first wife, and was understandably shocked when Leonard, out for a country walk with him and Virginia, fell behind to relieve himself. Eliot was self-conscious about the other allegation: 'The critics say I am learned and cold,' he told the Woolfs. 'The truth is I am neither.' It took three years before Eliot could be brought to call Leonard and Virginia by their first names. When he finally did relax he demonstrated that he could be human and humorous, as illustrated by the following acceptance of an invitation to tea:

Possum now wishes to explain his silence
And to apologise (as only right is);
He had an attack of poisoning of some violence,
Followed presently by some days in bed with laryngitis.
Yesterday he had to get up and dress—
His voice very thick and his head feeling tetrahedral,
To go and meet the Lord Mayor & Lord Mayoress
At a meeting which had something to do with repairs to Southwark Cathedral.
His legs are not yet ready for much strain & stress
And his words continue to come thick and soupy all;
These are afflictions tending to depress
Even the most ebullient marsupial.
But he would like to come to tea

One day next week (not a Wednesday)
If that can be arranged
And to finish off this letter
Hopes that you are no worse and that Leonard is much better.

Virginia thought that it was wrong for a poet with Eliot's talents to be forced to support himself by working for a bank, and in 1922, in co-operation with Lady Ottoline Morrell and Imagist Richard Aldington, attempted to create an Eliot Fellowship Fund with enough money to enable Eliot to leave the bank and spend his full time writing.* In the following year she campaigned, although unsuccessfully, to have Eliot appointed Literary Editor of the *New Statesman*. It finally became possible for Eliot to leave the bank in 1925, when he was made a director of the publishing firm now known as Faber & Faber. Virginia rather illogically felt he had deserted The Hogarth Press—obviously his writing thereafter would be published by his new associates—but soon forgave him and they remained friends.

In 1922 Leonard and Virginia met Vita Sackville-West and her husband Harold Nicolson. By the end of 1925 Vita was obviously in love with Virginia, and Virginia just as obviously was enthralled with Vita who reminded her of 'a guard's officer in bearskin and breeches'. Virginia's interest was not because of Vita's writing, which Virginia thought was produced with a 'pen of brass', but rather because of Vita's love of high adventure, her noble connections and her virile beauty, the essential elements of the traditional fairy tale. This fairy tale aspect of Vita is expressed on nearly every page of *Orlando* and so intrigued Virginia that, according to Quentin Bell:

Virginia felt as a lover feels—she desponded when she fancied herself neglected, despaired when Vita was away, waited anxiously for letters, needed Vita's company and lived in that strange mixture of elation and despair which lovers—and one would have supposed only lovers—can experience.

*   *   *

There may have been—on balance I think there probably was—some caressing, some bedding together. But whatever may have occurred between them of this nature, I doubt very much whether it was of a kind to excite Virginia or to satisfy Vita.

Nigel Nicolson's *Portrait of a Marriage*, which contains excerpts from the extremely frank correspondence between his parents, largely confirms Professor Bell's conclusions. Vita stated in a letter to Harold, 'I

---

* Virginia's witticism that if Eliot had stayed in banking he might well have ended up as a branch manager is implausibly cited by Lytton Strachey's biographer as proof that Virginia was jealous of Eliot. Holroyd, *Lytton Strachey*, vol. 1, p. 404.

110 *Angelica Bell, Clive, Virginia and Maynard Keynes in front of the lodge in Monks House garden – the room in which Virginia did much of her writing*

111 *Maynard Keynes in upper sitting room at Monks House*

112

113

114

115

112 *Lydia Keynes, of whom Virginia wrote: '. . . has the nicest nature in the world and a very limited headpiece . . . Her contribution is one shriek, two dances; then silence, like a submissive child, with her hands crossed.'*
113 *'the shriek' – Lydia Keynes with Virginia and Julian Bell*
114 *'the dance' – Lydia with Duncan Grant*
115 *'her hands crossed' – Lydia with Morgan Forster*

116

117

118

119

116 *T. S. Eliot at Monks House with Morgan Forster in a corner of the kitchen. Behind them hangs one of the three primitive paintings which the Woolfs bought in 1919 at the sale of the contents of Monks House. Forster was so fond of the picture that he later borrowed it from Leonard and hung it in his rooms at King's College, Cambridge*

117 *In the garden with Vivienne Eliot*

118 *In the upstairs sitting room*

119 *In the downstairs sitting room which, in warm weather, was sometimes used as a dining room. When Eliot saw this picture he wrote to Leonard: 'The look of rapt imbecility worries me; it is a warning of how I shall look in my dotage.'*

120 *Vita and Virginia in Monks House garden, 1933*

121 *Vita with Pinka in her lap in the upper sitting room at Monks House, 1932*

122 *Vita mounted on her donkey, Mouse, at the Plain of Malamir, Persia, in 1927*

123 *Vita and Leonard in Monks House garden, 1933*

124

1.

126

12

Some Monks House visitors

124 *Elizabeth Bowen*

125 *Lady Sybil Colefax*

126 *Dame Ethel Smyth*

127 *Stella Benson and Virginia*

128 *William Plomer with one of the garden statues*

129 *Virginia with James and Alix Strachey*

130 *Stephen Spender and his wife Natasha with a friend*

28

129

30

131 *Virginia bowling with Angelica, Quentin and a friend*

love Virginia—as who wouldn't? But ... one's love for Virginia is a very different thing: a mental thing, a spiritual thing, if you like, an intellectual thing ... I am scared to death of arousing physical feelings in her, because of the madness ... I *have* gone to bed with her (twice), but that's all.' This leaves open the question whether, as implied, Vita had never *tried* to arouse 'physical feelings' in Virginia or whether, if she had, there would have been any passionate response.

The hopelessness of pursuing Virginia must have been apparent to Vita at an early date. Nigel Nicolson says that 'The physical element in their friendship was tentative and not very successful, lasting only a few months, a year perhaps.' From Virginia's point of view, where there never seems to have been any 'physical element',* the attachment may have been longer. Whatever glamour Vita had for Virginia had worn thin by 1935 when she received a letter from Vanessa in Rome reporting on an encounter with Harold Nicolson, Vita and one of Vita's girl friends:

On the 24th the Nicolsons arrived & the next day we had to dine with them. I hadn't seen Vita for ages—she has simply become Orlando the wrong way round—I mean turned into a man with a thick moustache & very masterful & surely altogether much bigger—How have you done it? Perhaps its partly by contrast with her absurd little lover—who seemed as white as a sheet—quite unable to look after herself in any way—& altogether rather silly I thought. Harold always seems to me to be suffering severely from inferiority complexes but if one takes a lot of trouble to reassure him he gradually gets more at ease— & is rather a nice but foolish creature, I should think somewhat boring.

Vita was not the only glamour in Virginia's life. There were also her periodic excursions into Society: the literary and artistic gatherings of Lady Ottoline Morrell—that strange but magnificent woman given to passionate romance and extremes of coiffure, make-up and dress, 'got up to look precisely like the Spanish Armada in full sail', Virginia once put it; and the more formal parties of Lady Sybil Colefax and Lady Emerald Cunard. Leonard describes a party at Argyll House, the residence of Sir Arthur and Lady Colefax, attended by 'the Prime Minister and half the Cabinet, Mary Pritchard, Margot Asquith, the editor of *The Times*, Max Beerbohm, and Augustus John'. Lady Cunard, meanwhile, might be entertaining the Prince of Wales, the Duke of Kent, George Moore and Sir Thomas Beecham. Virginia had views of both salons, Leonard only of Argyll House.

These glimpses that Virginia had of Society reflect a wholly different aspect of her character: that of 'loving to cut a dash—to put on a smart

---

* ' ... it's a great thing being a eunuch as I am', Virginia wrote to Vita in 1927.

gown and go to a function, and then despising herself for it'. Intellectually, Virginia knew that the salons were pretentious, sterile and false; emotionally, she liked the excitement of meeting handsome people in handsome clothes. Indeed she liked parties of all kinds. But parties and glamour were not at all to Leonard's taste. He thought Lady Colefax was 'a damned snob'. He was more amused by the animals in the zoo — which he frequently visited — than by the guests at a fashionable party. He liked to read and listen to music, or to play chess or to argue with friends about politics or literature or life. He quoted Ben Jonson:

What a deal of cold business doth a man misspend the better part of life in! in scattering compliments, tendering visits, gathering and venting news, following feasts and plays, making a little winter-love in a dark corner.

That, Leonard said, expresses the view of every man who had reached the age of thirty-five and had lived in civilised society.

[10]

MALICE OR MISCHIEF?

132 *Virginia – a watercolour given by Vanessa Bell to Leonard Woolf,
Christmas 1935. Now at Monks House*

Virginia's love of glamour offers a clue to an important side of her com-
plicated nature: in many respects she remained a child all her life. Two
other clues pointing in the same direction were her lifelong need for a
mother figure, and her sexual immaturity. Her fun, also, to name still
another aspect, was often that of a child. Virginia's purchase of 'a green
glass jar from a chemist—one of those great flagons that glow or used to
glow in pharmacy windows—was for her, it having been coveted perhaps
since childhood, an event possibly as important as Katherine Mansfield's

friendship or the German air raids'. Gerald Brenan observed when Virginia was in Spain in 1923 that she was 'as excited as a schoolgirl on a holiday'. In 1928, when Virginia was 46, Vita wrote about her 'sweet and childlike nature'. Her conversation, Quentin Bell explains, 'was full of surprises, of unpredictable questions, of fantasy and of laughter—the happy laughter of a child who finds the world more strange, more absurd and more beautiful than anyone could have imagined possible.' Virginia's niece recalled that 'As often as not' her talk 'was of the more nonsensical sort, make-believe and speculation as to the goings on of people we didn't know, the sort of games one plays as a child.' Some of these child-like, nonsensical elements are illustrated by this fragment from a letter she wrote to Hugh Walpole in 1930:

I wish I could think of anything else to make you envious. I like printing in my basement best, almost: no, I like drinking champagne and getting wildly excited. I like driving off to Rodmell on a hot Friday evening and having cold ham, and sitting on my terrace and smoking a cigar with an owl or two.

Virginia liked children; not just in the abstract, she liked to be with them, and children loved her. They called Virginia by her first name as though she were one of them. She treated them as equals and joined in their undeclared conspiracies against parents. Once when she was alone with the young Nicolson boys and saw Vita approaching, she called out 'Go away Vita, can't you see that I'm talking with Ben and Nigel?' Her jokes were often children's jokes. Imagine the glee on the face of Barbara Bagenal's young daughter when, meeting Virginia in the street, the latter said to her: 'Will you come with me to Woolworth's to buy a very large india-rubber? I want to rub out all my novels.' And Quentin Bell has given a wonderfully amusing account of his aunt's conversation on a drive from Lewes to Sevenoaks: 'We met an elephant on the road here only the other day—I fancy they are common in this part of Kent. Why, there is another. Well, perhaps its only an old sow but you wouldn't usually find a sow that looked so much like an elephant in any other part of England.'

Child-like, yes; but a number of individuals, even some of her friends, said that she was 'malicious'. What is usually overlooked is that 'malicious', a favourite word in the Bloomsbury vocabulary, was most often used to mean mischievous or teasing, rather than malevolent. The milder sense was not limited to Bloomsbury; it was an accepted meaning at the time. The *Oxford English Dictionary* published in 1933 defines 'malicious' as 'Given to malice; addicted to sentiments or acts of ill-will. Now sometimes used in a milder sense: Given to sportive mischief;

inclined to tease.' And teasing was a favourite Bloomsbury sport. To give an example: Virginia's novel *Jacob's Room* contains the following passage as Jacob's mother wanders through a graveyard in Scarborough at the end of the day:

Yet even in this light the legends on the tombstones could be read, brief voices saying, 'I am Bertha Ruck', 'I am Tom Gage'. And they say which day of the year they died and the New Testament says something for them, very proud, very emphatic, or consoling.

To Virginia the name 'Bertha Ruck' probably was nothing more than an amusing sound. She did not know, although almost everyone else in England who read books seemed to know, that there was a popular writer of the day named *Berta* Ruck, author of *Arabella the Awful* and a great number of other novels with similarly appealing titles. Berta Ruck was definitely not buried in Scarborough but was very much of this world and living with her husband—the distinguished novelist Oliver Onions. Mr and Mrs Onions were extremely annoyed at what seemed to be this intentional slight to Miss Ruck's artistic skills, and a lawsuit was threatened. Virginia, however, managed to convince the Onions that she had never heard of Berta Ruck's books, although they were selling in far greater numbers than anything Virginia had written. She and Virginia became friends, and Virginia later spoke with admiration of the entertainment Berta Ruck had provided at a Bloomsbury party where she sang 'Never allow a sailor an inch above your knee'.

The story up to here is fairly notorious, having been included in most accounts of Virginia's life. A recently discovered letter provides a hitherto unreported addendum to the incident. After Virginia had received the irate communication from Berta Ruck and her husband, another letter addressed to Virginia arrived at Hogarth House. This letter was signed 'Thomas Gage'. It began:

Madam,
    My attention has been called to page 217 of your recently published novel, 'Jacob's Room', on which page you describe two tombstones inscribed with my name and the name of my honoured friend, Miss Berta Ruck.
    May I assure you that you are likely to have good reason to know that neither myself nor Miss Ruck are, as you suggest—and seem to wish— occupants of a graveyard at Scarborough, or elsewhere?
    Of your attempt to injure the literary reputation of the Authoress of 'Bridge of Kisses', & 'The Lad with Wings', and to clear from your path a literary rival, the circulation of whose books in England, the British Dominions, and the United States, you may hope in vain to equal, I say

nothing. Miss Ruck's lawyers will see to it that she receives adequate and conspicuous amends. Nor should I deign to speak of your use of my name with hers on contiguous tombstones, were it not that the perfidious juxtaposition has given rise to much unpleasant comment, which Miss Ruck is *too much of a lady* to speak of, but which I, as an English gentleman and member of the R.N.R. (retired) feel bound to protest against in no measured terms. Everyone who knows Miss Ruck knows that in her noble bosom there harbours no sentiment of which an angel could feel ashamed. But strangers outside the sacred circle of her acquaintances will receive a very different impression ...

Well before this point Virginia must have recognised the letter for what it was—a leg pull. Any doubt was removed by the claim, as the letter continues, that the incident 'has so gravely affected my health that I have been forced to resign my position as superintendent of the Lavatory at Oxford Circus ... '

Leg pull it was, but by whom? Leonard was certain the culprit was Logan Pearsall Smith who, because of some earlier practical joke, was automatically charged by Leonard with every new incident. Eventually the true culprits surfaced: they were Lytton Strachey and Dora Carrington.

Virginia was accustomed to being teased as well as to teasing—even the Woolf servants entered into the spirit of the game. The distinctive feature of Virginia's teasing is that it was almost always based on fantasy. Her most intimate friends knew that much of what Virginia said— particularly if it was funny—had to be discounted by a substantial percentage. A good example of this type of fantasy was provided by Virginia's play *Freshwater* which was a spoof on three famous Victorian figures: Tennyson, the poet Laureate; George Frederick Watts, the painter; and Julia Margaret Cameron, a pioneer photographer and great aunt of Virginia herself. From her earliest childhood Virginia had been hearing first-hand accounts of each of the three principal characters. She knew that Tennyson loved to read his poetry aloud, and particularly his poem *Maud*. She knew that 47-year-old Watts had married 16-year-old Ellen Terry (a most unsuccessful match since the marriage was never consummated) and that she was made to pose hour after hour wearing a white dress or veil, while 'Signor' worked on his allegorical paintings. And Virginia also knew all about her talented, eccentric and domineering great aunt, Julia Cameron. (A portfolio of the photographs taken by Mrs Cameron sold for £52,000 at a Sotheby auction in 1975.)

These ingredients she combined in a play that was supposed to take place, as its name suggests, at Freshwater on the Isle of Wight, where the Camerons, Tennysons and Watts were neighbours. The ageing Camerons are about to return to India where they had spent most of their married life. They cannot go, however, until the completion of their coffins, which they insist on taking with them. Tennyson, who has come over from Farringford to say goodbye, proposes to read *Maud* to them once again in the two hours and twenty minutes that remain before their departure. Ellen Terry, draped in a white veil, is posing for Watts, who is painting his famous allegory of Mammon. Mrs Cameron is imperiously commanding everyone to pose for her photographs. Interrupting Tennyson she says:

Alfred, Alfred, I seek Sir Galahad. Where shall I find Sir Galahad? Is there no gardener, no footman, no pantry boy at Farringford with calves—he must have calves.

After action involving the other players she returns:

What is the use of a policeman if he has no calves? There you have the tragedy of my life. That is Julia Margaret Cameron's message to her age! All my sisters were beautiful, but I had genius. They were the brides of men, but I am the bride of Art. I have sought the beautiful in the most unlikely places. I have searched the police force at Freshwater, and not a man have I found with calves worthy of Sir Galahad. But, as I said to the Chief Constable, 'Without beauty, constable, what is order? Without life, what is Law?' Why should I continue to have my silver protected by a race of men whose legs are aesthetically abhorrent to me? If a burglar came and he were beautiful, I should say this to him, Take my fish knives! Take my cruets, my bread baskets and my soup tureens. What you take is nothing to what you give—your calves, your beautiful calves—I have sought beauty in public houses and found her playing the concertina in the street. My cook was a mendicant. I have transformed her into a Queen. My housemaid sold bootlaces at Charing Cross: she is now engaged to the Earl of Dudley. My bootboy stole eggs and was in prison. He now waits at table in the guise of Cupid.

Since Virginia mentions Cupid, it should be explained that in actual fact Ellen Terry, bored with life at Freshwater, made an unscheduled appearance one evening and did a dance in front of the assembled company, which included some distinguished guests, dressed as Cupid in pink tights. If this were not bad enough, the story that later was repeated all over London was that she had appeared naked and danced on a table before a group of 'confused and astonished bishops'. The pink tights sealed poor Ellen's doom; the two great aunts of Virginia who had arranged the unconsummated marriage now arranged a separation and Ellen, by this time 17, was sent home to mother.

The above is fact. In Virginia's version, instead of pink tights, Ellen shocks Watts by wearing trousers at a meeting with a young man (John Craig) in the garden:

Watts: Miserable girl—if a girl I can still call you. I could have forgiven you much but not this. Had you gone to meet him as a maiden in a veil, or dressed in white, it would have been different. But trousers—no— ... Go then. Vanish with your paramour to lead a life of corruption—
Craig: Hang it all Sir. I have a large house in Gordon Square.*
Watts: Go then to Gordon Square. Found a society in which the sanctity of the marriage vow is no longer respected.

The coffins finally arrive for the Camerons and they leave. A moment later Tennyson's servants rush in with the message that Queen Victoria has driven over to see him. As the Queen is wheeled on, Tennyson says (to the audience, very grimly) 'The comedy is over'. He falls to his knees. Several phonographs play God Save the Queen and Curtain.

In 1935, when *Freshwater* was performed for a party of friends, Vanessa Bell played the key role of Mrs Cameron, Leonard Woolf was Mr Cameron and Duncan Grant was Watts. The parts of Lord Tennyson and Ellen Terry were taken by Julian and Angelica Bell. The cast studied their parts carefully and five rehearsals were held. When the play was produced in Vanessa's London studio, Clive Bell and his brother Cory laughed so loudly that some of the members of the audience complained that they couldn't hear the lines.

The kind of teasing that occurred in *Freshwater* caused no ill-feelings within the family and among old friends. New acquaintances, however, were often dumbfounded when Virginia took some innocent fact concerning them and built it up into a story they could hardly recognise. An example has come to light involving Gladys Easdale, the mother of Joan Easdale, a young poet whose works had been published by The Hogarth Press. The background facts seem to be these: Mrs Easdale had a son who was a musician; Virginia and Leonard had attended a concert at which his music was played; the mother had told Virginia that she had mentioned her son to Sir Henry Wood, famous conductor of the period. Mrs Easdale's recently discovered diary contains an account of what later occurred during tea at Monks House, beginning with these words uttered by Virginia to the assembled party:

'She is the bravest woman I know—she went into a big restaurant straight up to Sir Henry who was surrounded by a crowd of Ladies & said "Sir Henry my son is a genius!" now you go on with the story'—Naturally I was covered with

---

* Gordon Square was a favourite Bloomsbury address and, in particular, the home of Vanessa and Clive Bell since the time of their marriage.

confusion. Then she continued (in that charming playful way of hers) 'You see—she has a son who is an unknown distinguished composer.' Next she talked of the Recital—the most interesting she had ever been to—that we were the most advanced family in the world—setting to music words no one else would dare, & also the most modern of music—& all this carried on half serious half humourous.

Virginia's trick of blowing up a few facts into something quite different and then asking a bystander to 'go on with the story' was not uncommon with her, and while most people thought it was amusing, some thought it was cruel. It is obviously impossible to say for certain that Virginia meant only to amuse and did not realise that the victim might feel that she was being cruel, but in the instance above there is not the slightest doubt that Virginia was well-disposed toward the visitor. She had voluntarily attended the son's recital, the Press had printed the daughter's poetry, and they had exchanged several social visits. Indeed, the 'victim' of the teasing in this case took it all in obvious good humour. Not all victims felt the same. Dora Sanger referred to Virginia's 'merciless chaff' and said that Virginia, although 'reverential' to her husband, the saintly C. P. Sanger, had been 'cruel' to her. In contrast, Barbara Rothschild, in a letter to Leonard, asked him to 'tell Virginia that we long to see her too and to be led again into the tortuous and torturing mazes of indiscretions into which she lures the carrot followers'. Virginia's chaffing frightened some people, amused others. We know that although Virginia was conscious that she sometimes frightened people, she did not know why. 'I wish one day you would write and say why I frighten,' she wrote to Dorothy Bussy, 'I have every vice, I agree: but why my wretched ramshackle assortment of vices should put fear into the young and lovely and gifted, with all life before them ... Heaven knows.'

Virginia's unusual upbringing, without the confining structure of a formal education and without the abrasive lessons derived from learning to 'get along' in the harsh world, made it likely that she was not always conscious of her impact on others; that she set words loose without thinking of the harm they might do. At the same time it may have been partially responsible for her fresh perception of what she saw and felt; her enjoyment of small, inconsequential things on which the adult world sets little value; and her freedom from the obvious and trite. What Leonard called 'taking off'—using a prosaic incident or statement to create a baroque mountain of fantasy—was simply another manifestation of that child-like freedom from banality which was a part of her nature. This can be illustrated in many other ways. The smells of people are important in children's talk, but become a taboo subject for adults, whereas Virginia had no difficulty writing that Katherine Mansfield 'stinks like a ... civet cat'. The typical adult has been taught that jealousy is evil. Hypocritically, we try to hide that fundamental element of human nature, which exists in everyone short of the saints. But children who have not yet been educated into a stereotype will admit their jealousy — and Virginia time after time in her diary confesses that she is jealous: of women with children, of the writing of Katherine Mansfield or T. S. Eliot or Lytton Strachey, or of someone else who had had a success. To Virginia's friends these child-like traits: her gaiety and love of little things, her mischievousness, frankness, fantasy, freshness, were an essential part of the character they found so attractive.

[11]

THE PRIOR OF LEWES

133 *Head of Leonard Woolf by Charlotte Hewer, now in Monks House garden*

A few years before Leonard died he received a remarkable letter from one of his neighbours—a man born in Rodmell about the time the Woolfs had moved there in 1919. He had known Leonard all his life, and the letter was full of admiration: 'If I wanted some one', the letter read, 'who would speak truthfully and not be influenced by fear, it would be you.' The letter continued:

I think you are essentially a religious man ... a person who is not self indulgent, has a self imposed code of conduct with high moral standards, and a reverence for life in its many forms. In fact if you had lived in the Middle Ages you could well have been a Prior of Lewes Priory of somewhat unorthodox views but a capable and vigorous administrator of the Priory's lands and interests.

There is nothing in Leonard's papers to indicate what he thought of this letter, but it takes little knowledge of the man to be able to say with certainty that it would have pleased him very much.

Leonard *was* a religious man, although he acknowledged no formal religion. As we have seen, he was an unbeliever when he entered Cambridge but had attended synagogue until at least two months before his eighteenth birthday. 'He was a strict Jew as a small boy', wrote Virginia, 'and he can still sing in Hebrew'—presumably the first Jew to become one of the Cambridge type of Apostles. He was a student of both the Old and New Testaments, and in a heated exchange with the Archbishop of Canterbury claimed that his position on the issue under dispute was more compatible with the precepts of Jesus Christ than was the position taken up by the Archbishop. There never was a visible conflict between Leonard and Virginia over religion. She had been an agnostic from birth and was whatever Leonard was. 'We are Jews,' she once said. Leonard declared, 'as regards my Judaism, I know that it is strange that it should have had so little effect upon my life'. Leonard's younger brother Philip thought the family's religion had been a positive force, and expressed surprise that Leonard had not stressed this in his autobiography. While Leonard's sister Bella complained that he had failed to give adequate credit to their mother for the family's success, Philip complained that 'You gave no weight to the effect of our being Jewish'.

Leonard seems never to have replied to Philip's comment. Perhaps it was because he no longer thought in sectarian terms. We know that his religion—that is, the creed that guided his conduct and which he thought should guide the conduct of others—was founded purely on the relation of one man to another; it was devoid of any ritual, any priesthood, any theology, any conception of life after death, any tradition of miracles, saints or holy days. 'I feel passionately for what I call civilized life,' he wrote. Such a life, in Leonard's words, was a combination of the Semitic vision: justice, mercy and tolerance, with the Greek vision: liberty and beauty. His writings and his actions, throughout a long life, were governed by these precepts. He was a socialist but, unlike many other socialists in England, he would not condone deviation from the standards of justice, tolerance and liberty by a socialist government. A correspondent who credited Leonard with a 'liberal' point of view was corrected: 'I am not a Liberal and never have been one. Ever since I began to take any part in politics ... I have been a socialist. Where you go wrong is in thinking that freedom of thought is somehow or other a crime in a socialist and that socialism consists in a continuous mumbling and re-mumbling of phrases from Marx, Lenin and Stalin.'

The one area in which Leonard may have departed from his own creed was, strangely, tolerance. As an extreme rationalist, he could not tolerate attitudes based on instinct or emotion. As one who held strongly-felt opinions in certain fields of knowledge, particularly politics, he often could not tolerate views that differed widely from his own. In a letter to an old friend, a practising Christian, he wrote:

I admire and sympathize with much of the Christianity of Christ, although some of it is impractical and some nonsense. If he had brought me the Sermon on the Mount in 1920 I should have published it with the greatest pleasure (and would probably have been the only publisher in London who would have done so) and I am sure he would have been quite willing to be published by someone with my views. What I don't like is the Christianity of the Churches, of the Archbishop of Canterbury, Queen Elizabeth II, the Pope, and the Moderator of the Church of Scotland which worships respectability and a synthetic deity composed of 90% Mammon and 10% God.

Beatrice Webb describes a 'raging argument' with Leonard and Virginia* 'about denominational education and the validity of religious mysticism'. According to Mrs Webb, 'they were against toleration—what was "manifestly false" was ... not to be thought by persons above a certain level of intelligence who claimed to be honest with themselves and other people'.

Leonard was not content to hold to his own disbelief and to allow others to believe; he had a missionary's zeal to destroy the belief of others and to convert them to the Truth: that is, to his way of thinking. Approximately ten pages of the first volume of his autobiography were devoted to an attack on formal religion. He wrote that he 'could not understand how any intelligent person of the twentieth century could get himself in the frame of mind in which praying to God meant something to him'. He was filled with 'silent amazement' to see T. S. Eliot go to communion at the Rodmell village church. 'I could, if pushed to it', Leonard wrote, 'produce an intellectually adequate explanation of the psychological process that brought Tom into the respectable fold of the Church of England, but I have no sympathetic understanding of it.' The scorn Leonard displays toward the 'respectable' nature of the

---

* Leonard claimed that Virginia and Sidney Webb remained silent during the debate.

church, here and in the earlier quotation, tells us much about Leonard himself. So does the fact that he seems far more offended by Eliot's departure from rationality as demonstrated by his church attendance, which is so underscored in Leonard's autobiography, than he was by Eliot's departure from rationality as shown in his slight anti-semitism, which Leonard does not even mention, although he was conscious of it. In response to an inquiry, Leonard wrote: 'I think T. S. Eliot was slightly anti-semitic in the sort of vague way which is not uncommon. He would have denied it quite genuinely.' To another correspondent he added: 'In conversation and every day life he did not in my presence, at any rate, ever show any signs of it. I think we must have discussed it, but I do not remember with what result.'

There were other subjects, in addition to religion, on which Leonard felt passionately and which were sure to trigger off a passionate response from him. When Mrs H. M. Swanwick, a co-worker for many years on behalf of the League of Nations, wrote a book called *Collective Insecurity* in which she argued against the usefulness of sanctions, she was bitterly attacked by Leonard who strongly believed in them. The attack was not only on the point at issue but also a personal one on Mrs Swanwick who, among other things, was accused of 'self-satisfied complacency'—a charge which Leonard made publicly in the *New Statesman*, and for which he subsequently expressed regret in a personal letter.

Margaret Cole's book *The Story of Fabian Socialism* received extremely rough handling by Leonard in a review he wrote of it for the *Political Quarterly*, and the author, with whom Leonard had worked for more than thirty years as a fellow Fabian, was given a thorough trouncing. Leonard pointed out that Margaret Cole and her husband Douglas had 'revolted' against the Webbs in the Fabian Society and that a reader of the book 'gets the feeling of not being able to see the Webbs ... for the Coles'. The author's 'personal prejudice', said Leonard, 'makes her judgments and even sometimes her facts unreliable.' Her writing was attacked as 'continually slovenly'; and the review ends on this shrill note: 'if any English master wants a sentence on which he can lecture to his form on "how not to write the English language" he could not do better than take as his example the monstrosity which fills the first nineteen lines on page 163'. An extended correspondence ensued between 'Dear Leonard' and 'Dear Margaret'. Margaret finally received the limited satisfaction, if satisfaction it was after the public lambasting, of having Leonard declare to her privately that 'I ought not to have reviewed the book', presumably because of his own personal involvement in the early Fabian squabbles. The reason he did review it, a practical one, was even less satisfactory: 'I wanted to read it [the book], but being a publisher and ex-literary editor, I never buy books, and am apt to review a book if I want to read it,' he confessed truthfully.

The Life of John Maynard Keynes by Roy Harrod, which has since become something of a classic in its field, was another recipient of a review by Leonard (in this case an unsigned one) that in retrospect seems unnecessarily harsh, although the personal element was less of a factor. At two points in the review the book was called a 'failure' and the author's literary style was castigated as 'naïve', 'uneasy' and 'wordy'. In a letter written years after the event, Harrod expressed his displeasure with Leonard's review. Leonard replied, 'I ought never to have reviewed it and am quite prepared to believe that I did not do it justice. But I was not spiteful ... I don't think that spite is one of my many vices. Irritation and an irritable pen or typewriter are, and there are certain things in your book which irritated me, as the review showed ... But you had grounds for being angry with me.'

One cannot help wondering why, in these instances, Leonard had so obviously forgotten the advice he had given others when he was Literary Editor of the *Nation*: that the most effective slating is one that is the most impersonal. One suspects the existence of a character trait, a sense of insecurity, that was as deeply rooted in Leonard as immaturity was in Virginia—possibly related to the loss, in each case, of a loved parent during childhood. Leonard's self-conscious creation of a carapace at an early age to serve as protection against a 'hostile world' is eloquent testimony to the presence of that insecurity. His attacks on formal religion and his repeated expressions of contempt for the 'respectability' of the church has the odour of defensiveness. Despite his acknowledged intellectual powers, Leonard was an outsider in the Apostles and was conscious of it; no other member of that society ever wrote at such length of his association with the group. Leonard was an outsider in the Foreign Service who found it necessary, even in his later years, to assure himself over and over again of his unusual competence in the work he had performed in Ceylon a half-century before. The same need, presumably, impelled him to write to a friend 'I claim to be more serious and more intelligent than the average person'. He even felt himself to be, in a sense, an outsider in his relations with his own family, a feeling reflected in the statement, made when he was past 75, that his mother had loved him less than any of her other children. A sense of insecurity would also go far to explain the resentment Leonard seemed to express, in his reviews, toward the intrusion of lesser authorities into fields in which Leonard felt especially competent, and to explain the stubbornness with which he defended positions that he had taken in the past. 'It was useless to argue with him,' said Keynes. This flaw was minimised by the care with which Leonard studied a subject before arriving at his conclusions. His conclusions were usually right, but his methods of expression often failed to persuade. The reviewer of *Quack, Quack!* in *The Listener* found Leonard 'too passionate and too bitter to be the perfect exponent of the quiet methods of discussion which he advocates'. The minutes of the Labour Party's International Advisory Committee for a meeting held on January 11, 1928 read: 'The toning-down of Mr. Woolf's Memorandum [on the Outlawry of War] was left to the Chairman and the Secretary.'

To his friends, Leonard's proverbial stubbornness transcended the limits of mere irritation—it became an amusing eccentricity,* like his care with money or his record-keeping. When he wrote a book he maintained a log in which he recorded the number of words written each day. Such facts as the first frost of the winter, the elapsed time for driving from Monks House to Tavistock Square, the number of miles driven each year, Virginia's health, the date he had his hair cut, the bushels of apples yielded by each tree in the Monks House orchard, where the wild flowers of Sussex could be found and at what dates, his expenditures in every category, and the principal events of the day for nearly every day over a period of more than fifty years, were the kinds of information he compiled; a wonderful compendium of data for someone who enjoyed argument and liked the support of incontrovertible proof.

From what has been said it might appear that Leonard was an unpleasant person with a solemn view of life. Neither was true; even people who thought him difficult to work with found Leonard courteous and charming. He was a considerate and amusing companion, a good host and a good guest. Although there is only one known photograph of him smiling or laughing, his attitude toward life was dry and laconic rather than solemn. In describing one of his family as 'a dyed in the wool Woolf', he meant one who surveys 'the world and its inhabitants with reserve, suspicion, and resignation'. These characteristics Leonard had in full measure, but he also had a good sense of humour, as demonstrated by these sentences from an early review:

If you read old numbers of *Punch*, you will find that it must have been quite a common thing for Victorian old gentlemen to call a policeman if a small boy put his tongue out at them on the king's highway. That was an idiotic thing to do, and I am tempted to draw from it some profound reflections upon the social psychology of an age which was finally and fitly destroyed by the late

---

* Leonard's references to his own obstinacy suggest that he may even have regarded it as a virtue.

war. I doubt whether there is a single old gentleman in London who to-day would pay any attention — far less think of a policeman — if a street-boy put his tongue out, and the result is that there is no small boy in London who ever thinks it worth his while to put his tongue out at old gentlemen.

Scattered throughout his writings are similar examples of a nice wit. There is the letter in which he tells a correspondent, 'I am glad you take my advice, although I don't always take it myself', and the entry in his diary which reads, succinctly, 'pruned trees and my finger'. He possessed, too, a marked gift for describing people in a few disarmingly simple but very apposite words. Thus Bertrand Russell was a crusader 'remarkable for his great courage, immoderation, and sometimes contempt for consistency. He is in fact a mixture of Socrates, Don Quixote and Puck.' 'Rudyard Kipling was a genius and like many other geniuses, a rather nasty man.' Nor were Leonard's colleagues on the *New Statesman* spared such revealing characterisations. Of Clifford Sharp, one-time editor, he wrote: 'I acquired an affection for Clifford Sharp, but it was the kind of affection which one sometimes gets for an old, mangy, bad tempered, slightly dangerous dog. One is too rather proud of being among the few whom he will with a growl allow to pat him gingerly on the head.' And of Kingsley Martin, another editor of that weekly, he said: 'Kingsley's mind was not tuned to eternity and the music of the spheres, but to a period of exactly a week.'

Leonard could be caustic as well as witty in his correspondence, particularly if the point at issue involved some cause about which he had strong feelings. One of the causes that specially concerned him was the steadily increasing encroachment of new building on the South Downs after the First World War. He remembered the day when there were no buildings between Newhaven and Brighton except for a combined Post Office and tea room at Telscombe Cliffs. The rash of post-war speculative building at Peacehaven appalled him. Moreover he and Virginia had suffered severely from the cement plant constructed at Asheham. In 1968 he was disturbed by a proposal to build another cement plant near Mt Caburn. He wrote to the East Sussex County Council:

If chalk for cement works is required, I suggest that it should be obtained from in and around Peacehaven where the scenery might be improved by substituting cement works for the existing buildings.

When John Lehmann was engaged in writing his book about the Sitwells called *A Nest of Tigers*, Leonard wrote, 'I hope your use of the word nest in the title means that you are showing what they were — cuckoos in tigers' clothing.' Leonard was also able to laugh at himself.

In the 1940s he received a letter from a Ceylon citrus planter who identified himself as the husband of a girl Leonard had found attractive nearly
forty years earlier when he himself was in Ceylon. She appears in
Growing as 'Gwen' where she is described as 'pretty, lively, sweet-
natured and I became fond of her and she of me.' Contemporaneous
evidence suggests that there was more than fondness. In 1907 one of
Leonard's letters to Strachey says: ' ... it so happens that I am really in
love with someone who is in love with me.' The fact that she had grown
extremely heavy in the interval between 1907 and 1943 may have had
some dampening effect on Leonard's recollection of his relations with
the girl.

The renewal of contact by 'Gwen's' husband was occasioned by a
manual he had written on citrus culture. He had sent it to Leonard hop-
ing that it might be published by The Hogarth Press. Leonard declined
it but perhaps not sufficiently firmly, for the author sent several more
copies of the manual directly to The Hogarth Press offices, where they
came to the attention of John Lehmann, then acting as general manager
of the Press. When Lehmann asked Leonard to brief him, he received
this reply:

The position is this. [The author] is a boring Ceylon planter. I do not know
him at all. But when I was 25 and his wife was 17, we had an absurd, amusing
and romantic affair in the first station I was sent to in Ceylon. I thank God
that I have never seen her again as I believe she now weighs 22 stone. On the
strength of this, he wrote to me some imbecile letters asking me to publish this
book in the Hogarth Press ... despite my recollection of [her]—I gave him a
direct refusal ... It is monstrous that the sins of one's youth should be visited
upon one in the shape of a Citrus Manual 40 years later.

Leonard's type of quiet humour was not at all strange to Virginia.
Except for the subject matter, particularly the last, the examples quoted
above might have been taken from the writings of her father. 'At one of
my meetings', wrote Sir Leslie Stephen about his discussions with
Matthew Arnold, 'I do remember a remark which was made, and which
struck me at the moment as singularly happy. Unfortunately, it was a
remark made by me and not by him.'

[12]

THE HOMEMAKERS

134 *The downstairs sitting room, Monks House*

Although Virginia was pre-eminently a novelist of ideas she was, surprisingly, one of the few novelists who have written about the homely facts of day to day living: about housework, sewing, shopping, pouring tea, servants, keeping household accounts. These were not simply subjects for fiction; Virginia had struggled with them all. The small leather Address Book which she kept next to the telephone at Monks House contained not only the number of the Nicolsons at Sissinghurst Castle but also those of the butcher, the fishmonger, the laundry and the grocer.

While Virginia's own account of her experiences at the cooking school which she attended in 1914 suggests that her sole distinction was managing to cook her wedding ring into a suet pudding, she was, nevertheless, able to bake bread, make cakes and marmalade, as well as to cook a variety of straightforward dishes. When, in 1917, she wrote to Vanessa that 'my books run to about 17s. a head' she was not speaking about the books she was writing or reading. She was referring to the accounts of household expenditure, those terrible books that had caused so much trouble in the Stephen family. And Virginia kept them, at least during the early years of her marriage, as Vanessa and Stella and Mrs Stephen had in days gone by.

Virginia was far from adept with the needle. Her underclothes, as she confessed, were often pinned together by brooches, an embarrassment that deterred her from shopping for dresses. In an emergency Virginia could clumsily sew things, as she did after Bob Trevelyan burned out the seat of his trousers while crouched before the fireplace reading his poems aloud. Her inadequacy in this field was the subject of some annoyance when she contemplated the shining skills of Vanessa. After watching a visitor at Monks House darn stockings in 1939, Virginia was amazed to find she could do it herself. She cried out, 'Oh Leonard, look! Wait till Vanessa sees what I've done!'

An entire volume could be written about Virginia's experiences with servants, particularly those two stalwarts: Nelly Boxall and Lottie Hope, who began working for the Woolfs in 1916. In those days servants were in some respects very much a part of the family. Thus it was possible for Lottie to remain in the Woolf household for another six years after Virginia recorded in her diary that 'Lottie and Leonard twit each other about their bad tempers'. At one moment Lottie was reported to be a 'wild ass' or an 'intoxicated Jay' and at another as 'perfectly angelic and as humble as a caterpillar'. When Lottie was ill she wrote to Virginia 'long letters, from friend to friend'. A few months later 'she made a mouse out of marzipan with a tail of string' which she put in Virginia's cup at teatime.

Nellie had problems with her teeth. Then she was run over by a car but, like a hen, emerged unhurt. When she and Lottie had German measles they were waited on by Leonard and Virginia. The two girls spent their savings on dancing lessons; were agnostics like Leonard and Virginia; read opened letters that were left around, and carried the household gossip horizontally to the Bells' servants at Charleston or Gordon Square, and vertically to the clerks in the solicitors' office on the floor below the Woolf residence in Tavistock Square. It is hardly surprising that Virginia thought fondly of 'an enchanted world, where I turn a handle and hot mutton chops are shot out on a plate—human agencies entirely ignored'.

More than once Leonard and Virginia quarrelled about the servants; Leonard was ordinarily very much in favour of a harder line with them than Virginia was willing to take, and she frequently had to salve feelings wounded by an abrasive comment or two from Leonard; although there were occasions when Leonard had to do the salving. There were other quarrels, too, in the Woolf household. Possibly the largest single cause of dispute was the strict regime Leonard established for Virginia, and the closely related question of whether she should attend a gathering where she would encounter people Leonard thought too provocative for her. Leonard had doubts, especially, about the kind of party Clive Bell or Ottoline Morrell were likely to give.

There was tension also in their games of bowls, played on the lawn at Monks House. In a series—one might almost call it a tournament—that began in 1935 and continued for six years, they played over 1,200 games. Virginia was a keen competitor, as she was in everything she undertook. She hated to lose to Leonard at bowls; but lose she did, time after time. In fairness to her it must be recorded that although the Monks House lawn was not exactly a perfect bowling green, there were various dips and hollows in it unlikely to be noticed by one who had not run a mower over it. Perhaps Virginia claimed that she was victorious more often than was justified by the facts, or maybe it was only a reflection of his inveterate record-keeping habits; but whatever the reason, Leonard conscientiously recorded the outcome of every game he played with Virginia. This he converted into annual totals, as the table shows.

	V	L	Draw
1935	8	42	
1936	57	174	1
1937	59	177	
1938	47	178	
1939	84	222	
1940	73	259	3

In the circumstances, one cannot be surprised by this entry in Virginia's diary for June 22, 1940: 'I've been beaten at bowls, feel depressed and irritated and vow I'll play no more.' Yet she did play more—and continued to be beaten.

Since their discussions covered every kind of subject, they found plenty of areas for disagreement. A remarkable instance of being able to disagree without being disagreeable to each other is provided by Virginia's 22-page essay 'Reviewing', published by The Hogarth Press in 1939, to which Leonard appended a five-page note stating that some of Virginia's conclusions 'seem to me doubtful because the meaning of certain facts has been ignored or their weight underestimated'. Has there ever been such an example of husband and wife calmly stating their different points of view in public? Yet there were instances of acrimony: 'Leonard says we owe a great deal to Shaw. I say that he only influenced the outer fringe of morality ... [that] the human heart is touched only by the poets. Leonard says *rot*, I say damn. Then we go home. Leonard says I'm narrow. I say he's stunted.'

Virginia was normally able to accept Leonard's views on political or economic issues. 'Alix [Sargant-Florence] and Fredegond [Shove] to dinner' begins Leonard's diary for January 6, 1918. 'Talked about Tolstoyism. Gerald [Shove] has given up smoking because it's an indulgence. V said we ought to give up all our capital. I said it was non-sense.' In 1930 when Virginia wanted to improve the interior of Monks House and Leonard wanted to spend money on the garden they settled the issue by splitting the costs so that Virginia bore the expense of the interior improvements, amounting to £454 odd, and Leonard bore the expense of the changes in the garden amounting to some £80. The £17 cost of moving the garden W.C. was divided equally between them.*

Obviously these were not the only differences that arose in their twenty-eight years of married life, but they are typical of the kind of arguments they had and the kind of settlements they arrived at. Leonard saw Virginia as formidable and knew that she could sometimes come perilously close to a breakdown. He may, on occasion, have simply held his peace when there was a disagreement. That practice seems to be reflected in the following entry in Leonard's diary for April 1, 1920: 'Found a cuckoo flower out in the fields, & equisetum pushing up in the dykes, V says it is the oldest flower of the world a doubtful state-ment. Cowslips fully out among the willows.'

The material aspects of the Woolfs' domestic life were dictated by elements peculiar to their situation: Virginia's health, Leonard's job, their income. Because of Virginia's need for periodic rest and relaxation

* When Leonard and Virginia came upon better times, the excess of total income over basic living costs in each year was divided equally and became a personal 'hoard' to be used in any way the individual might wish. During the period 1924–39 the total amount split in this way was in excess of £18,000.

135 *Monks House as it was in 1919*

136 *As modified beginning in 1927, principally by adding a bathroom and a two-room extension at the extreme left*

137

138

139

137 *Seen from the garden. Here the dormer windows of the extension are at the right. This was the location of the upstairs sitting room, where most of the indoor Monks House photographs were taken. Virginia's bedroom was immediately below, opening into the garden*

138 *Garden statuary and one of the three garden ponds*

139 *The garden front as it is today with the lean-to glasshouse added in the 1950s*

140

141

142

140 *Monks House from the garden. The block-like extension housing the upstairs sitting room and Virginia's bedroom can be plainly seen*

141 *A view of the garden from the house*

142 *The house from the garden as it is today*

143

14

145

146

143 *Winter at Monks House. Monks House was bought as a summer and weekend residence. It had no central heating. Its clapboard walls provided slight protection against the winds off the Channel. Unusually low temperatures and heavy snows were encountered during the winters of 1939 and 1940*

144 *Leonard skating on the pond in Monks House garden*

145 *Virginia's Lodge in the garden, where she usually wrote when she was at Rodmell*

146 *The garden, with the lodge and church in the middle distance, as it is today*

171

they had to have a place in the country, and because of Leonard's work they had to have a residence in or near London. The houses had to provide working areas for two people, for none of the jobs held by Leonard required more than two or three days a week at an office; the rest of the time he worked at home. Despite their small income they managed to maintain two residences from the outset. For the first two-and-a-half years of London life (1912–15) they rented rooms in Clifford's Inn and then in Richmond. Thereafter they occupied houses: they were at Hogarth House in Richmond from 1915 to 1924; at 52 Tavistock Square from 1924 to 1939; and at 37 Mecklenburgh Square from 1939 on. Their Sussex home from 1912 to 1919 was at Asheham, a house off the Beddingham-Newhaven road, and from 1919 on at Monks House, Rodmell, approximately half-a-mile as the crow flies on the other side of the Ouse river. On average, about one-fifth of their time was spent in the country during the 1920s and about one-third during the 1930s. Going from the city to the country was no simple matter before the Woolfs bought a car: 'We travel with a selection of our books packed in hampers,' wrote Virginia in 1923. 'Add to this a dog and a tortoise, bought for 2/- yesterday in the High Street. My husband presides with considerable mastery—poor devil, I make him pay for his unfortunate mistake in being born a Jew by discharging the whole business of life.'

The cost of living at the Tavistock Square and Mecklenburgh Square houses was considerably reduced by letting the ground and first floors to a firm of solicitors (the basement was used by The Hogarth Press). So the Woolfs' part of these premises was frugally limited to the two top floors. None of the houses occupied by the Woolfs can be regarded as very grand: Monks House was bought for £700 and the Mecklenburgh Square house, to which they moved in 1939 at the height of their prosperity, had been a boarding house before they rented it. The cost of maintaining two houses (including rent, rates, utilities, insurance, heat, household supplies, etc.) was £190 in 1917, £243 in 1927 and £388 in 1937. And then there were the servants: two girls for most of the time (for a short while three, and often less than two) whose wages in total averaged about £80 annually over the whole period. Food was always the major item of expense; the Woolfs entertained a great deal and it was important to keep Virginia's weight up. In 1917 they spent £232 on food, which was a fair amount those days. However, in the next twenty years the annual cost of food never exceeded £320.

These items—house, servants and food—represented their main outgoings for a long time. The total spent on doctors in 1917 was £15, which included 9 guineas paid to Dr Harrison, the Woolfs' dentist.

This was a typical distribution of their medical costs: in nearly every year the expenditure on dentists was greater than on doctors. In 1917 Virginia spent £32 on clothes, including four dresses costing 18 guineas, a cloak for one guinea, and miscellaneous small amounts for combinations, stays, shoe repairs, gloves, etc. Leonard's expenditure on clothes in 1917 included such items as a suit for £5 10s. 2d., a sponge for 6s. and a stud for 6d.—every penny accounted for.

The furnishings in the Woolf houses were extremely simple. Some of them seem to have come from 22 Hyde Park Gate. There were, however, no valuable pieces of furniture. If there ever had been such heirlooms, Vanessa must have disposed of them in 1906 when she moved the family out of Kensington. In the early days of their marriage, china had to be borrowed whenever a party was given. At the auction of household effects that followed the sale of Monks House to them in 1919, the Woolfs bought in 30 or so Lots, all useful objects, on which they spent a total of £20 odd. Typical items were twelve bone-handled knives and six forks for 19s., twelve kale pots for 7s. and a sheep-dipping platform and trough for 2s., although there is nothing to indicate they ever kept sheep. The only other expenditure that might be deemed frivolous was the four shillings spent on 'three old panel oil paintings' which still hang in Monks House today. Relatively little furniture was acquired later. The largest single item bought during their first ten years at Monks House appears to have been a sofa, purchased in 1926 for £8 10s.

There were five areas in which the Woolfs indulged themselves once their financial situation began to improve in the late 1920s. First came a series of modest improvements to Monks House which testify to the extreme simplicity of their living: a bathroom with lavatory was added in 1927 to replace the earth-closet used during their first seven years of ownership. Electricity was introduced in 1931, and the house was connected with the water main in 1934. The cramped quarters within the cottage were expanded by adding two small rooms in 1930: a new bedroom for Virginia and a sitting room. Four years later a lodge was constructed in the garden as a work room for Virginia.

There was some furniture purchased for the rooms added in 1930: 'For years I never had a pound extra; a comfortable bed, or a chair that did not want stuffing,' wrote Virginia in her diary. 'This morning Hammond delivered 4 perfectly comfortable armchairs—and we think very little of it.'

Bookshelves were built and the spaces not occupied by books were gradually covered with pictures, principally those of Vanessa Bell, Duncan Grant and Roger Fry. In the Tavistock Square House, wrote

Virginia, 'my rooms are all vast panels of moonrises and prima donna's bouquets—the work of Vanessa and Duncan Grant'. The fireplace, mantelpiece and walls were all painted by them. The table and four chairs, inscribed with Virginia's initials, that ended up at Monks House, and the several hand-made rugs with Vanessa/Duncan designs—circles and cross-hatching—were apparently part of the original decor of that room. Tiles made by Vanessa and Duncan were a feature of the fireplaces in the new rooms added to Monks House in 1930, and are still there.

In July 1927 Leonard bought his first car: a second-hand and somewhat decrepit Singer which Vita understandably called the 'old umbrella'.* They paid £275 for the car, and its operating costs ran to about £100 a year. About the same time a full-time gardener was employed at £2 a week plus a cottage. The gardener, Percy Bartholomew, stayed on for nearly twenty years, quarrelling with Leonard over almost every gardening decision made during that period. Leonard's idiosyncrasies were related each night at the Bartholomew family dinner table, beginning with the words 'Woolf has been spuddling around again', whereas Bartholomew's peculiarities, as related by Leonard, were a continual source of amusement to Leonard's friends. Leonard estimated that the net cost of the Monks House garden in 1928 was £20 a year, after crediting the value of the fruit and vegetables which the Woolfs themselves consumed. When they were in London, Bartholomew shipped a weekly hamper to Tavistock Square by train.

The final indulgence was in foreign travel. For the first ten years after their honeymoon they stayed at home. In 1923 they made a brief visit to Gerald Brenan in Spain. In 1925 they went to France. Then, beginning in 1927 and for the next twelve years (except for 1930 and 1938) they regularly went abroad. These trips were in fact hardly more of an extravagance than the 'old umbrella'. They never stayed in first-class hotels, or ate in expensive restaurants. The most the Woolfs spent on any of their trips (the visit to Greece in 1932) was £166. For the purpose of Leonard's idiosyncratic accounting system this was recorded as £147, since he always deducted the estimated cost of meals, presumably on the sensible theory that they would have spent that amount on food if they had stayed at home. On these foreign trips Virginia was ill on only one occasion: when at Vanessa's suggestion she took a sea-sick pill to which she proved allergic.

There never seems to have been any disagreement between Leonard

* The car was replaced in 1930 with a new Singer. Three years later a Lanchester was acquired which was driven for the next twenty-two years.

and Virginia about their mode of living. They both were naturally frugal. As we have seen, Virginia spent little on clothes. She smoked cheap Belgian cigarettes and later switched to cheap cigars. Her little luxuries were in things like writing pens, or coloured papers, and later a clothes' allowance for her niece Angelica. Virginia was chided by Clive Bell for her dowdy appearance, and she occasionally borrowed things from Vanessa. In 1921 she wrote: 'I've had an accident with my only dress.' In the following year: 'I can't forever appear in the same skirt.'

Leonard far out-did Virginia. He used printer's proofs for toilet paper; Raymond Mortimer claims that he actually found sheets of Virginia's typescript 'heavily corrected with her pen' that had been put to that use. And when the paper shortage became acute in the early days of the Second World War Leonard adopted the practice, which he never abandoned, of re-using the envelopes of letters he had received in the post. And the reverse sides of letters written to Leonard were used by him for the carbon copies of letters he himself wrote.

They seldom bought spirits or wine.* Virginia drank coffee and tea, and was a large consumer of milk. They were great readers, devouring books, to use Virginia's expression, 'as a weevil ... eats cheese', but didn't spend much on them. They did occasionally buy books, and enjoyed picking over second-hand bookstalls; but mostly they subscribed for books through the Times Book Club or borrowed them from friends or from the London Library, which at the time of Virginia's death showed nine books on loan to her. There were a great many books in the house, but the valuable ones were those inherited from Leslie Stephen or presentation copies of books written by friends. And of course there were endless review copies, not all of which were sold. Books were spread about in all the rooms. Many were on the shelves, but others were on tables, chairs and floors; they were piled up on either side of the staircase so that a person going up or down could find enough space for only one foot at a time. Virginia's room was an 'incredible muddle of objects'. Neither Leonard nor Virginia was bothered by the disorder that prevailed in their houses. The animals they had, and they included a marmoset as well as a succession of dogs, added to the clutter. When they later acquired a cat, the rooms were 'further crowded by tin dishes on the floor'.

Not long after their marriage Leonard and Virginia were occupying separate bedrooms. Virginia had her breakfast in bed, brought to her on a tray by Leonard. They wrote in the mornings. In the afternoons when

* Late in life Leonard developed a taste for good wine; his wine bill in 1965, for example, exceeded £250.

they were in London they often worked at The Hogarth Press, particularly in the early days. At Monks House they walked, or Virginia walked and Leonard gardened. Although most evenings were spent at home, they both liked the theatre and listening to music. Early in 1913, before Virginia's illness manifested itself, they attended no less than fourteen operas or concerts, seven theatrical performances, and two art exhibitions in a period of four months. In later years, when they had a gramophone and wireless and Virginia's outings were being curtailed, they reduced their attendance at public performances to an average of about one every two weeks. Evenings at home, when they were alone, were ordinarily spent before an open fire reading and listening to music.

Were Leonard and Virginia happily married? A character in one of Virginia's novels would almost surely reply with another question — What is happiness? Perhaps a fair way to approach this issue, rather than to explore the meaning of happiness in an absolute sense, is to ask whether Leonard and Virginia would have been happier if they had married someone else or not married at all. As to Virginia, the answer to this question seems quite clear. At the end of her diary for 1919 she wrote, 'I daresay we are the happiest couple in England'.* In 1922 she stated plainly, 'I couldn't have married anyone else.' In the letter she left for Leonard on the mantelpiece on March 28, 1941, she said, 'I owe all the happiness of my life to you ... I don't think two people could have been happier than we have been.' But it is not necessary to rely on these statements for an answer. Virginia from early childhood was a lonely person, and Leonard, in the words of one of Virginia's heroines, 'destroyed' her loneliness. There was no one else who had both the intelligence that could be respected by Virginia and the strength and forbearance to support and protect her for the twenty-eight years they lived together. Leonard provided the conditions under which she was able to write, and this was Virginia's overwhelming interest in life.

The only regret she had — and this introduces the question of Leonard's happiness — was her inability to have children: 'Never pretend', Virginia reminded herself in her diary, 'that the things you haven't got are not worth having ... Never pretend that children, for instance, can be replaced by other things.' This desire for children may have weakened with the passage of time. But to the extent it ever represented a frustration it was due to Virginia's own physical condition and not to the choice she made of a husband. It can in no way affect Quentin Bell's conclusion

* 'Saxon ... talked a great deal about marriage ... and said how our marriage seemed the best of any he knew, and how coming to see us one night, he had understood for the first time the advantages of being married.'

that her decision to marry Leonard was 'the wisest decision of her life'.

Leonard must have had the same regret about children. But in his case there was a second regret. Their sex relationship was one that would have unnerved many a less resolute character. What had been a passive attitude by Virginia at the outset shortly developed into a complete affirmative rejection of the sexual act. Thereafter they lived 'chastely', so Virginia told Gerald Brenan when they visited him in Spain in 1923. Virginia suffered from no delusions about her condition: 'poor Billy', she wrote of herself, 'isn't one thing or the other, not a man nor a woman.' It is also quite possible that, from a personal point of view, she did not regret her frigidity. Her view may have been expressed by Mrs Dalloway, who though a wife and mother, 'could not dispel a virginity preserved through childbirth which clung to her like a sheet'. Mrs Dalloway 'resented it'—the thing she called 'this cold spirit'—and the explanation is that it was 'a scruple picked up Heaven knows where, or, as she felt, *sent by Nature (who is invariably wise)*'. In short, that her frigidity may have had a good purpose. What purpose? Perhaps to avoid any distraction from her art. There is no point in discussing the source of this 'scruple' in Virginia; maybe it was the advanced age at which she married,* or the erotic advances of Virginia's half-brothers while she was young, discussed at some length in Quentin Bell's biography; or simply Virginia's physiology. But whatever its origin, the 'scruple' makes it especially difficult to answer the question whether the marriage was a happy one for Leonard. And we must remember that we are attempting to find an answer for Leonard, who loved Virginia, and not for any other individual or for the average man. The answer, we are disposed to think is 'yes'—it was a happy marriage for Leonard. It could have been happier than it was; not if Leonard had married someone else, but if Virginia had been other than she was.

---

* 'The long abstinence from sexuality to which they [women] are forced and the lingering of their sensuality in phantasy have in them, however, another important consequence. It is often not possible for them later on to undo the connection thus formed in their minds between sensual activities and something forbidden, and they turn out to be psychically impotent, *i.e.* frigid, when at last such activities do become permissible,' *Collected Papers* by Sigm. Freud (1925), vol. IV, pp. 211–12.

147

147 *Woodcut by Diana Gardner, one of the residents of Rodmell, depicting the German aircraft that machine-gunned Monks House in 1940*
(Sussex Express & County Herald *January 9, 1942*). *Courtesy Diana Gardner*

148 *These two great elms on the edge of Monks House garden were known as 'Leonard' and 'Virginia'. Virginia's ashes were buried beneath the tree that bore her name. Two years later the tree was blown down in a huge storm*

[13]

MONKS HOUSE EXILES

148

The Second World War had an immediate impact on the lives of Leonard and Virginia. In August 1939, the month before Germany invaded Poland, the Woolfs had moved The Hogarth Press and their personal possessions from one Bloomsbury address to another—from 52 Tavistock Square, where they had lived for fifteen years, to Mecklenburgh Square. When the war broke out, they decided to make their principal home in the country, at Monks House, going up to London once a week and occasionally spending a night or two at Mecklenburgh

179

Square. This pattern continued for about a year—until September 1940 —when the London house was badly damaged by a bomb during the Battle of Britain. As a consequence, the winter of 1939–40 was spent mostly in Rodmell, while the winter of 1940–41 was spent wholly there, with none of the occasional nights in London.

Monks House had been acquired as a weekend and holiday residence. The principal feature was its lovely setting in the Sussex Downs, over-looking the water meadows of the Ouse Valley. Even in good weather it was never a comfortable house, and in cold weather it was extremely uncomfortable. Unlike most Sussex houses it was built mainly of wood, and the winds, to which it was exposed on all sides, blew through it freely. The sitting room had a red brick floor that oozed moisture. The house had no central heating. To get from Virginia's bedroom to the bathroom and lavatory it was necessary to go out into the garden, down a few steps into the kitchen, through a hall and up a flight of stairs to the first floor. There was another lavatory in the garden, which was not much more convenient and considerably less attractive. Rodmell seldom sees any snow or ice, but the winters of 1939–40 and 1940–41 were an exception. On December 19 Virginia's hand was so cold she couldn't hold a pen. It snowed on December 28, 1939 and the following night the temperature fell to 27° F, so Leonard was able to skate on the pond in the garden. There was snow and skating throughout January 1940 and it snowed heavily again in February. Virginia, who 'hated to feel cold at any time; it seemed to affect her in a strange way—almost to frighten her', wrote in her diary, 'the wind cuts like a scythe; the dining room carpet is turning to mould'. She came down with the 'flu and was laid up in bed until the end of March. In the following winter the snow held off until January, when it was followed by some very cold weather. Virginia wrote: 'The house is damp. The house is untidy. But there is no alternative.'

It should not be imagined that Virginia, because of her record of periodic depression, was constantly living at the edge of her nerves. True, she disliked cold and found that noise disturbed her work. But there are many perfectly normal people who do not like cold or noise. Virginia was not the typical fidgety introvert. In ordinary circumstances she was calm and reserved. Virginia was 'so still, so alert' at concerts that she was called, by one observer, the 'frozen falcon'. She was even calm under quite extreme conditions. During air raids in the First World War she kept the servants laughing with her jokes until Leonard urged her to stop so that he could sleep. Leonard's niece, Philippa Woolf, recalls staying at Monks House when Leonard's pet marmoset, Mitz, jumped on to Virginia's head and fixed her claws in Virginia's hair so firmly that she could not disentangle herself, nor could she be removed by either Virginia or Philippa. Virginia sat and talked with Philippa for over half an hour, quite calmly, while the marmoset clutched at her hair, until Leonard returned home and managed to disengage his pet.

Virginia's distress during the winter of 1940–41 was not the result of nerves in the usual sense. It was the result of a host of circumstances, of which the weather was only an incidental factor. By the end of June 1940 a seemingly invincible German army had conquered Poland, Norway, Denmark, Holland and Belgium and swept through northern France, driving the British out of Dunkirk, to stand fifty miles from the Sussex coastline. Rodmell is due south of London, only four miles from Seaford bay, and on the path of German bombers headed for the capital. The first air raid warning in Rodmell sounded on August 8, 1940. From then until November 13, a period of three months, air raid warnings were a regular feature, night and day; in some instances as many as six in a 24-hour interval. Dog fights went on overhead. A Messerschmitt shot down on Mt Caburn looked like 'a settled moth'. On several occasions German planes flew low directly over the house: 'They came very close. We lay down under the tree. The sound was like someone sawing in the air just above us. We lay flat on our faces, hands behind head. Don't close your teeth, said L. They seemed to be sawing at something stationary. Bombs shook the windows of my lodge. Will it drop I asked? If so, we shall be broken together.' At night the windows of Monks House shook when bombs were dropped on London, the London that was Virginia's personal treasure. 'Eight of my city churches destroyed' she wrote on January 1, 1941, and two weeks later she recorded 'the desolate ruins of my old squares: gashed; dismantled; the old red bricks all white powder … all that completeness ravished and demolished'. Rodmell was also immersed in the land war. The village had refugees from both London and Dunkirk. Hospital trains carried their sad burdens on the tracks that ran along the river bank. Barbed wire and pill-boxes were erected on the Monks House grounds. 'A strong feeling of invasion in the air. Roads crowded with army wagons, soldiers,' wrote Virginia. Rodmell could have been overrun in a first wave of any invasion. 'Capitulation will mean All Jews to be given up. Concentration camps. So to our garage.' In the Monks House garage a supply of petrol was kept 'for suicide should Hitler win'. Adrian Stephen had also given them lethal doses of morphia so they could avoid being taken prisoner. 'I can't conceive', Virginia wrote in June 1940, 'that there will be a 27th June 1941.'

Food became difficult to find. This, of course, was a problem for everyone, but it was crucial to Virginia's health. 'How one enjoys food now', recorded Virginia at the end of 1940, 'I make up imaginary meals.' This then was Virginia's situation in 1940 and 1941. One could hardly conceive of a worse one for a person whose sanity depended on keeping away from excitement, having sufficient rest, and getting plenty of nourishing food. And unfortunately, the pressures from the outside coincided with enormous internal pressures. In May 1940 Virginia had finished her biography of Roger Fry, who had died in 1934, a book that she did not want to write but did so only because of the urging of Roger's sister, Margery Fry, and of Roger's mistress, Helen Anrep. Simultaneously, Virginia had been writing *Between the Acts*. As always, the writing excited her, and as always the excitement was followed by depression. This time there were some important differences. First, Leonard's regimen of calm, rest and good food could not be followed. Second, Virginia was tortured by the thought that since she had gone mad in the First World War it was likely that the same thing would happen during the Second.

Leonard saw the danger signs. Visits to doctors in 1913 had alarmed Virginia rather than allayed her fears. So we can be certain it was no coincidence that Octavia Wilberforce, a doctor practising in Brighton, came in 'for tea' on December 9 and again on December 23. She brought gifts of milk and butter from her farm. She began drawing Virginia out and as soon as she returned home set down the conversation in letters to her friend Elizabeth Robins. Virginia told her about the difficulties she had had over the Roger Fry biography: how agents of J. P. Morgan had asked Maynard Keynes to intervene for the purpose of effecting a deletion from the biography of portions dealing with Morgan and his mistress, and about other criticisms she had received. Virginia said she 'had been sorting papers. Love letters from her father to her mother. Had been swept away by them. "Poor Leonard is tired out by my interest in my family and all it brings back."' Later, Virginia said that she had received 'irreparable blows' on the death of her mother and her half-sister Stella; that her father had 'made too great emotional claims upon us and that I think has accounted for many of the wrong things of my life ... I never remember any enjoyment of my body'. When Octavia asked what she meant, Virginia said, 'you adored the woods and games—I never had that chance', on which Octavia commented: 'It was all for her I gather intellectual and emotional—no healthy hunting outdoor outlet.' Reporting the same conversation, Octavia added: 'She so actively both loved and hated at the same time her father. Thought it a contribution that psychologists had explained that this was possible.' Virginia's hands, reported Octavia, were 'worse than icicles'. The 'teas' continued. Octavia came again three times in January and once in February. After the February visit she reported that Virginia 'looks a better colour but is still as thin as a razor'. Up to this point Virginia had been claiming (as she characteristically did when she was ill) that there was nothing wrong with her, but at tea on March 12 she finally confessed that she had been 'feeling desperate—depressed to the lowest depths, had just finished a story. Always felt like this—but specially useless just now.' Octavia commented to Elizabeth Robins: 'During part of the last war was when she lost hold and I've a feeling back of my head that she's a bit scared this may happen again.' Octavia had also thought that Virginia had looked 'almost scared' at the first tea on December 9, 1940. There was another tea on March 21 at which Virginia told Octavia that her two biographies, *Orlando* and her book on Fry, were 'failures'; that she could no longer write: 'I've lost the art ... I'm buried down here— I've not the stimulation of seeing people. I can't settle to it'; and that she 'had taken to scrubbing floors when she couldn't write—it took her mind off.' Virginia's floor scrubbing was a reflection of an overpowering restlessness. She was exhausted but refused to stay in bed. She lacked the usual diversion of friends, theatre, concerts. She found it impossible to lose herself, as she so often had in the past, in her writing. She looked for other work: the village authorities rejected her request to serve as a night fire-watcher, so she turned to the most menial tasks around the house. Vanessa, alarmed by the accounts she had from Leonard, begged Virginia to rest. If she did not, then a complete breakdown might occur at a difficult time: 'What shall we do when we're invaded', Vanessa wrote on March 20, 'if you are a helpless invalid.' This suggestion, in the circumstances, could not have been a consoling one. Surely the last thing Virginia wanted was to be a helpless invalid caught up in the invasion that seemed so imminent.

A week later, on March 27, Leonard called Octavia and asked her (she was sick in bed at the time) to see Virginia that afternoon. The story of what took place is touchingly told by Quentin Bell:

The interview was difficult. Virginia at once declared that there was nothing the matter with her. It was quite unnecessary that she should have a consultation; she certainly would not answer any questions.

'All you have to do,' said Octavia, 'is to reassure Leonard.' Then she added that she knew what kind of symptoms Virginia felt, and asked to examine her. In a kind of sleep-walking way Virginia began to undress and then stopped.

'Will you promise, if I do this, not to order me a rest cure?'

'What I promise is that I won't order you to do anything that you won't think it reasonable to do. Is that fair?'

Virginia agreed and the examination continued, but not without many protests. She was like a child being sent up to bed. In the end she did confess some part of her fears, fears that the past would come back, and that she would be unable to write again. Octavia replied that the mere fact that she had had this trouble before and that it had been cured should be reason for confidence. If you have your appendix removed, she said, nothing will remain but the scar; a mental illness can be removed in the same way if you don't inflame the wound by dwelling upon it.

At the end she took Virginia's hand, a cold thin hand she found it, saying: 'If you'll collaborate I know I can help you and there's nobody in England I'd like more to help.' At this Virginia looked a little happier—'detachedly pleased,' as Octavia put it.

Then there was a private consultation between Octavia and Leonard. What were they to do; should Virginia be under the surveillance of a trained nurse? It might easily be a disastrous measure. It seemed, both to Leonard and to Octavia, that the consultation had done some good. The Woolfs went back to Rodmell and Octavia returned to bed. She wrote Virginia a note, as gentle and as reassuring as she could make it, and on the following evening rang up, but by that time it was too late.

On the morning of Friday 28 March, a bright, clear, cold day, Virginia went as usual to her studio room in the garden. There she wrote two letters, one for Leonard, one for Vanessa—the two people she loved best. In both letters she explained that she was hearing voices, believed that she could never recover; she could not go on and spoil Leonard's life for him. Then she went back into the house and wrote again to Leonard:

> Dearest,
>
> I feel certain I am going mad again. I feel we can't go through another of those terrible times. And I shan't recover this time. I begin to hear voices, and I can't concentrate. So I'm doing what seems the best thing to do. You have given me the greatest possible happiness. You have been in every way all that anyone could be. I don't think two people could have been happier till this terrible disease came. I can't fight any longer. I know that I am spoiling your life, that without me you could work. And you will I know. You see I can't even write this properly. I can't read. What I want to say is that I owe all the happiness of my life to you. You have been entirely patient with me and incredibly good. I want to say that—everybody knows it. If anybody could have saved me it would have been you. Everything has gone from me but the certainty of your goodness. I can't go on spoiling your life any longer.
>
> I don't think two people could have been happier than we have been.
>
> V.

She put this on the sitting-room mantelpiece and, at about 11.30, slipped out, taking her walking-stick with her and making her way across the water-meadows to the river. Leonard believed that she may already have made one attempt to drown herself: if so she had learnt by her failure and was determined to make sure of it now. Leaving her stick on the bank she forced a large stone into the pocket of her coat. Then she went to her death, 'the one experience,' as she had said to Vita, 'I shall never describe.'

Tuesday.

Dearest.

I feel certain that I am going mad again. I feel we cant go through another of those terrible times. And I shant recover this time. I begin to hear voices, & cant concentrate. So I am doing what seems the best thing to do. You have given me the greatest possible happiness. You have been in every way all that anyone could be. I dont think two people could have been happier till this terrible disease came. I cant fight it any longer, I know that I am spoiling your life that without me you could work. And you will I know. You see I cant even write this properly. I cant read. What I want to say is that I owe all the happiness of my life to you. You have been entirely patient with me & incredibly good. I want to say that — everybody knows it. If anybody could

149 *Virginia's last letter to Leonard*

When lunch was ready and Virginia did not appear, Leonard found the notes she had left him. It was too late. By the time he reached the Ouse there was no sign of Virginia. Later that day, after all efforts to find her had failed, Leonard wrote a note which, creased and worn, was found among his effects when he died twenty-eight years later. It read:

They said: 'Come to tea and let us comfort you.' But it's no good. One must be crucified on one's own private cross.

It is a strange fact that a terrible pain in the heart can be interrupted by a little pain in the fourth toe of the right foot.

I know that V. will not come across the garden from the lodge, and yet I look in that direction for her. I know that she is drowned and yet I listen for her to come in at the door. I know that it is the last page and yet I turn it over. There is no limit to one's own stupidity and selfishness.

150 *Stephen Tomlin's head of Virginia Woolf, in Monks House garden*

[14]

AN EPILOGUE

Leonard Woolf was sixty years old at the time of Virginia's death in 1941. He lived another twenty-eight years. During the first nineteen years of that period he produced only one book—*Principia Politica*—as contrasted with the seventeen books he had written during Virginia's lifetime. But in 1953 Leonard began work on his autobiography. For unknown reasons he stopped after he had finished about a third of what was to become the first of five volumes. The work was resumed in 1958 and was again left unfinished. In January 1959 he began once more. The first volume was published in 1960 when Leonard was eighty years old. From then until the end of his life in 1969 a large part of his time was devoted to writing the remaining four volumes at the rate of 400 to 600 words a day, to answering fan mail and responding to requests for interviews, articles and broadcasts stimulated by the success of the books. The five-volume work as a whole must be considered the triumph of Leonard Woolf's long career. It is a great social document, describing what may prove to be the most critical period of British history, a period that saw the shattering of some ancient British institutions and the undermining of others. It is a great personal document, describing Leonard's loving care of Virginia, his founding of The Hogarth Press, and his graceful decline into old age.

In 1966 Leonard received a letter from the Prime Minister, Harold Wilson, stating that he had 'it in mind on the occasion of the forthcoming list of Birthday Honours to submit your name to The Queen with a recommendation that Her Majesty may be graciously pleased to approve that you be appointed a Member of the Order of the Companions of Honour'. In answering, Leonard said, 'I have always been (heretically) against the giving and accepting of honours and have often in the past said so. Much as I appreciate your kindness, I cannot therefore accept it, but I hope that you will not think the worse of me. Years ago Ramsay MacDonald offered the same honour to Virginia, and, sharing my views, she asked to be forgiven for not accepting it, and I drafted her reply in much the same words as I am now using for my own.'

Something that meant far more to Leonard was the dinner given for him on his eighty-sixth birthday, November 25, 1966, by the Cambridge Conversazione Society in the private dining room at Kettners Restaurant in Romilly Street. Wearing his 'purple tweeds in the midst of all the smooth dark suits', his 'rugged profile' looking 'like the head of Zeus', he spoke to his fellow Apostles of the euphoria, the happiness which begins at seventy and grows steadily greater as one advances into old age.

Leonard was able to work in his beloved garden until the summer of 1969. It was open to the public, in accordance with custom, on June 28. His diary entries cease after that date. He began running a high fever which did not respond to medication, and on August 14, nearly eighty-nine years old but reluctant to die, took leave of the world. He may, perhaps, in those last moments have recalled the lines he so often had quoted since his days at Trinity College:

> From too much hope of living,
>   From hope and fear set free,
> We thank with brief thanksgiving
>   Whatever gods may be
> That no life lives for ever;
>   That dead men rise up never;
> That even the weariest river
>   Winds somewhere safe to sea.

PARTICULARS OF THE
MEMBERS OF THE
MEMOIR CLUB

BELL, CLIVE (1881–1964). Trinity College, Cambridge. Married Vanessa Stephen in 1907. To the surprise of his friends, who had always looked on him as an interloper in Bloomsbury, Bell's first book, *Art*, published in 1914, was a great success, going through eight editions by 1927. It gave him at this early date an enviable position as arbiter of taste in the artistic world. Although he wrote a number of other books, none achieved the popular success of the first.

BELL, VANESSA (1879–1961). Eldest daughter of Sir Leslie Stephen. A painter, she attended the Royal Academy Schools and, for a brief time, the Slade. She exhibited at the Second Post-Impressionist Exhibition held in London in 1912. In 1964 a memorial exhibition of her painting was held by the British Arts Council.

FORSTER, E. M. (1879–1970). King's College, Cambridge. Morgan Forster achieved an international reputation through the publication of five novels that are still in print and widely read: *Where Angels Fear to Tread* (1905), *The Longest Journey* (1907), *A Room With a View* (1908), *Howards End* (1910), and *A Passage to India* (1924).

FRY, ROGER (1866–1934). King's College, Cambridge. Although trained as a scientist, Fry became a painter and an authority on art. He refused the directorship of the National Gallery in 1906 because he had accepted an appointment as curator of paintings at the Metropolitan Museum in New York. In 1913 he founded the Omega Workshop to employ artists who were unable to support themselves by their paintings. His public recognition occurred only near the end of his life following his appointment as Slade Professor of Art at Cambridge in 1933, and through his enormously popular lectures on art, which began in the late 1920s. He had married in 1896 but it soon became apparent that his wife was suffering from an incurable mental ailment. In 1910 she was removed to a retreat where she remained until her death in 1937.

GRANT, DUNCAN (born 1885). First cousin of Lytton Strachey. Studied in Paris under Jacques-Emile Blanche in 1906 and later at the Slade School. He, too, exhibited at the Second Post-Impressionist Exhibition in 1912. The Tate Gallery, which owns more than twenty of Grant's paintings, arranged an exhibition of his works in 1975, in recognition of his ninetieth birthday.

KEYNES, JOHN MAYNARD (1883–1946). King's College, Cambridge. During the First World War Keynes was given the responsibility of handling Britain's external debt. In 1919 he created a stir throughout the western world by resigning as Treasury representative at the Versailles Conference in protest against the harsh terms imposed on Germany. Within four months after his resignation he published his views in *The Economic Consequences of the Peace*, which was reprinted four times between December 1919 and April 1920. The works on which Keynes's world-wide reputation as an economist rests — *A Treatise on Money* and *The General Theory of Employment, Interest and Money* — were published in the 1930s. In 1925 he married the Russian ballerina Lydia Lopokova. He was made Lord Keynes in 1942.

MacCARTHY, DESMOND (1877–1952). Trinity College, Cambridge. Married Mary (Molly) Warre-Cornish in 1906. A journalist and editor, MacCarthy began writing reviews and dramatic criticism as a free lance. In 1920 he became Literary Editor of the *New Statesman*, signing his own contributions to it 'Affable Hawk'. Later he founded the magazine *Life and Letters*, and eventually became senior literary critic of the *Sunday Times*. He was knighted in 1951.

MacCARTHY, MOLLY (1882–1953). Daughter of F. W. Warre-Cornish, vice-provost of Eton. She wrote a novel that was published in 1918, *A Pier and a Band*, and in 1924 published a delightful account of her early years in Eton, *A Nineteenth Century Childhood* — almost certainly a product of her Memoir Club readings.

STRACHEY, LYTTON (1880–1932). Trinity College, Cambridge. Strachey's *Eminent Victorians*, published in 1918, became an instant success in Britain and the United States and the source of endless controversy concerning the four characters portrayed in it. This was followed, in 1921, by his *Life of Queen Victoria*, on which his reputation as a biographer chiefly rests.

SYDNEY-TURNER, SAXON (1880–1962). Trinity College, Cambridge. Sydney-Turner took a double first at Cambridge and did well enough in the Civil Service examinations to gain one of the choice openings in the Treasury. There he remained, sphinx-like, until his retirement. Despite his acknowledged brilliance, he could not make decisions, even to the extent of saying what was on his mind. 'We liked and admired him', one of his friends declared, 'for the things he never quite said.'

WATERLOW, SYDNEY (1878–1944). Trinity College, Cambridge. He married (1) Alice Pollock and (2) Marjorie Eckard. Waterlow entered the Foreign Service after leaving Cambridge, later went on to become the British Minister successively at Bangkok, Addis Ababa, Sofia and Athens. He translated into English several of the plays of Euripides and wrote a life of Shelley. He was knighted in 1935.

REFERENCES

CHAPTER I : THE EARLY YEARS

For an explanation of the abbreviations used in these references, see Note, p. 205

page
1 'The servants' Leonard Woolf, *Principia Politica* (1953), pp. 31–2
2 'an eager and a nipping air' 1 LW 28
2 'very nervous and highly strung' 1 LW 25
2 'seemed to be roughly' 1 LW 28
2 'toughness and sternness' 1 LW 16
2 'I loved your mother' Florence Abrahamson letter, September 25, 1964 (S)
2 'I think he was' 1 LW 25
2 'from my very early years' 1 LW 89
2 'The main outlines' 1 LW 22
2 At a *New Statesman* board meeting Conversation with V. S. Pritchett, 1975. Presumably Leonard was referring to 'public' apology, since several instances occurred in which he apologised by private letter.
2n hurt himself accidentally LW letter to Cecil Woolf, July 26, 1962 (S) acknowledging receipt of supplement to *The West London Observer* for April 23, 1897, p.1
3 A favourite card game Bella Woolf letter, March 23, 1952 (S)
3 There was a family newspaper Flora Woolf letter, September 14, 1960 (S); *The Lady*, January 1, 1959, pp. 8–9
3 'When the day came' 1 LW 39
3 from a 'small boy' 1 LW 66
3 'I habitually sat' 1 LW 53
7 'It is he' G. K. Chesterton, *Autobiography*, Hutchinson (1936) p. 71
7 'Clever and should do well' St Paul's School report on work from January to July 1898 (S)
7 'I was lamentably intelligent' 1 LW 89
7 'She loved all' 1 LW 33
7 'I know that it was' 1 LW 42–3
8 In his description of her *The Wise Virgins* (1914) pp. 167–8, 257–8, 305
8 his mother was outraged VW letter 637 (August 8, 1912)
8 he unfairly failed to give credit Bella Woolf letters, November 13, 1959 and November 21, 1959 (S)
8 'as a protection' 1 LW 71

9   'A word or even a look'   F. W. Maitland, *The Life and Letters of Leslie Stephen* (1906) pp. 23, 24

9*n* 'I am, like my father'   Maitland, p. 433

10   'as some people do to gin'   VW letter 203 (December 22, 1904)

10   'Mr Leslie Stephen'   Reprinted in *Stephen versus Gladstone* Headington Quarry (1967)

19   'These great people'   VW letter 371 (July 20, 1907)

19   'dressed in our best'   F. S. Oliver letter to VW, November 6, 1926 (S)

19   'his chair perilously'   Mollie Panter-Downes, *The New Yorker*, April 15, 1967

19   awkward presence   VW letter, 733 (October 25, 1915)

19   'were all tall'   F. E. Halliday letter, March 23, 1964 (S)

20   break down and cry   1 QB 40

20   'there is very little need'   VW letter 48 (August 1902)

20   'I went to a dance'   VW letter 259 (January 16, 1906)

25   clumsy erotic fumblings   VW MSS MH/A5a (S) and 1QB 43

25   'that house of all the Deaths'   Leon Edel, *Henry James, The Master*, Hart-Davis (1972) p. 392

25   'one of those strange'   1 LW 128

25   'in white dresses'   1 LW 183–4

CHAPTER 2: THE APOSTLES

page

27   'It is necessary'   1 LW 129

28   'most of the people'   *The Autobiography of Bertrand Russell* 1872–1914 Allen & Unwin (1967) p. 68

28   'Let us hope'   Maitland, p. 47

29   'for the active member'   *Walter Leaf (1852–1927) Some Chapters of Autobiography* (1932) p. 90

29   Before breaking up   Russell, p. 113

29   'The social conditions'   LW letter to Kingsley Martin, January 20, 1965 (S)

29   'envious and jeering'   *Autobiography of Charles Merivale* (1899 ed.) pp. 80–1

29   'We took ourselves'   Russell, p. 69

29*n* 'about the early years'   Christopher Layton letter, July 31, 1969 (S)

30   'was one of'   paper read by Dennis Proctor at annual meeting of July 25, 1970

30   'the spirit of'   A. S. and E. M. Sidgwick, *Henry Sidgwick A Memoir*, Macmillan (1906) p. 34

30   'It was a principle'   Russell, p. 69

30   the toasts were   R. G. Hawtrey letter, June 11, 1922 (S)

30   Barthold Niebuhr   Frances M. Brookfield, *The Cambridge Apostles* (1906) p. 8

32   forensic devices   J. M. Keynes, *Two Memoirs*, Hart-Davis (1949) p. 85; 1 LW 137

32   'It was this clarity'   1 LW 147

32   'had two important defects'   *The Listener*, June 9, 1949, p. 993

32 'some babies got thrown away' Pamela Diamond letter, February 14, 1965 (S)

32 'I didn't want' 2 QB 215

33 'personal affections' G. E. Moore, *Principia Ethica*, CUP (1903) p. 189

33 'we recognised' *Two Memoirs*, pp. 98, 82

33 flatly denied Keynes's statement 1 LW 148

34 'going through' Holroyd, *Lytton Strachey The Unknown Years*, Heinemann (1967) p. 208

34 'he looks pink' Holroyd, p. 213, 216–19

34 'homosexual relations' Russell, p. 74

34 seems to have become an active homosexual see Terminal note, p. 235, E. M. Forster, *Maurice* (1971)

34 'Saxon can't decide' VW letter 500 (August 8, 1909)

34 'We not only' *Walter Leaf*, p. 85

34 'the tie of attachment' *Henry Sidgwick*, p. 35

CHAPTER 3: THE APOSTLES IN BLOOMSBURY

page

36 'the Bloomsburians' A supplement to the *Oxford English Dictionary*, OUP (1972) p. 298

36 'very slapdash and jocular' VW letter 754 (April 22, 1916)

37 'Vanessa looking at a map' (and all following quotations about life in Bloomsbury until the letter to Lytton Strachey) VW MSS MH/A 16 (S)

41 'ap-s-les' VW letter 617 (May 21, 1912)

41 'nothing in the whole world' VW MSS MH/A5a (S)

41*n* '*sexual* relations bore me' VW letter to Jacques Raverat, October 3, 1924 (S)

CHAPTER 4: AN APOSTLE IN THE JUNGLE

page

43 'George or George or Both?' May 9, 1903, MSS (S)

44 'what Papa was' 1 LW 192

44 standing 69th *The Oxford Magazine*–Supplement. October 26, 1904, p. 2

44 'The best that I could hope for' 1 LW 194

44 'I am in a horrible state' LW *Letter to G. E. Moore*, October 4, 1904 (S)

45 'embittered and disappointed youth' 2 LW 172

45 'arrogant, conceited, and quick tempered' 2 LW 56

45 hardened his heart 2 LW 172–3

45 'I work, God, how I work' LW letter to Strachey, October 2, 1908 (S)

45 'Whenever I came new' 2 LW 107–109

46 'This was extraordinarily rapid' 2 LW 170

46 'In the 2¾ years' 2 LW 180

51 'A large crowd' LW *Diaries in Ceylon 1908–1911*, Hogarth Press (1963) 185

CHAPTER 5: COURTSHIP AND MARRIAGE

60   Virginia loved Vanessa's children   VW letter to W. A. Robson, July 26, 1937 (S): 'her children are like my own'

60   'Mama' and 'foster parent'   VW letters 197 (November 30, 1904) and 201 (December 11, 1904)

60   'treated like a nice child'   VW letter 272 (June 1906)

60   baby kangaroo   See VW letters 83 (June 4, 1903) written when her father was dying and 295 (November 14, 1906) written when her brother was dying

60   Vita 'lavishes on me'   2 QB 118, from AWD(B) December 21, 1925

60   'odd and remote'   2 QB 175

61   'longing to be in love'   Strachey letter to LW, August 21, 1909 (B)

61   'vehemently'   VW letter 608 (March 1912): 'Now I only ask for someone to make me vehement, and then I'll marry him!'

61   'As I told you brutally'   VW letter 615 (May 1, 1912)

61   'it's the voyage out'   *The Wise Virgins* (1914) p. 315

61   'I am in love with Aspasia'   undated MSS (S)

62   'She was . . . avid for affection'   J. R. Noble, editor, *Recollections of Virginia Woolf by her Contemporaries*, Peter Owen (1972) p. 84

62   time after time in her letters   See e.g. VW letters 38, 50, 62, 78

62   'Dearest and most beloved'   LW letter May 24, 1912 (B)

62   she 'loved' him   LW diary for 1912: May 29

62   The hallowed circle   Virginia found Leonard 'very like Thoby ... not only in his face', VW letter 631 (June 24, 1912)

62   'What do you think'   Letter from Bobo Mayor, May 26, 1964 (S)

66   Leonard wrote to G. E. Moore   LW letter, June 7, 1912 (S)

66   Virginia wrote to Violet Dickinson   VW letter 620 (June 4, 1912)

66   A joint note   VW letter 623 (June 6, 1912)

66   Duckworth wrote to Leonard   George Duckworth letter, September 8, 1912 (S)

66   nobly wrote to Leonard   Walter Lamb letter, June 4, 1912 (S)

66   Leonard had withdrawn £105   acct. Bk, p. 83 (S)

66   'a daily char came in'   3 LW 86

67   Leonard started to keep   LW diary for 1913

67   'Nothing you have ever done'   VW letter 679 (August 4, 1913)

67   'Dearest, I have been disgraceful'   VW letter 680 (August 5, 1913)

67   'I want you Mongoose'   VW letter 678 (August 3, 1913)

68   'I'm lonely without you'   LW letter, March 13, 1914 (S)

68   'She says the most malicious'   2 QB 26

69   In 1917, for example   LW diary for 1917

69   An incident that occurred in 1917   Conversation with Barbara Bagenal, 1975

70   'Now what *will* they say'   AWD 46

70   'I fail to see why'   undated MS 'Poetry & Prose' (S)

70   the average working woman in Great Britain   Based on absenteeism from work due to their own illness and accident. See Table 27, *Social Trends*, no. 4, 1973 HMSO

70   'collapses into bed'   2 QB 248

70   '*such* a liar'   2 QB 117n

71 'I am a very poor creature' Letter G. F. Watts to Leslie Stephen, April 2, 1896 (Sc)

71 'I believe these illnesses' AWD 153. This language is quoted by Sir George Pickering who accepts, without any analysis of the facts, that Virginia Woolf was a manic-depressive. Pickering, *Creative Malady* (1974) p. 287

71 And one cannot help noting Virginia herself (although surely her mathematics was faulty) seemed to have perceived a ten-year cycle: 'every ten years, at 20, again at 30, such agony of different sorts possessed me that ... I did most emphatically attempt to end it all.' VW letter 1337 (December 25, 1922)

71 'Normally, my wife' LW letters to Frank Fish, October 23, 1966 and November 4, 1966 (S)

71 Lady Oxford wrote Letter, May 4, 1941 (S)

71 Elizabeth Robins Letter, August 18, 1941 (S)

71 Professor William A. Robson Conversation, 1975

74 Virginia's nephew and biographer Conversation, 1970

74 'I think perhaps 9 people out of ten' AWD (B) September 13, 1919

CHAPTER 6: CAREERS: YEARS OF ANXIETY

page

75 would support themselves by writing VW letter 628 (June 1912)

76 'rather less than £400' 3 LW 90

76 'take a small house' VW letter 628 (June 1912)

76 letter from Alec Waugh July 22, 1965 (S)

81 the author's royalties 3 LW 89

81 She is bound by *The Wise Virgins*, Hogarth Press (1914) pp. 120, 148

81 'I feel there will be' Marie Woolf letter, December 11, 1913 (S)

81 Harry Davis has *The Wise Virgins*, Hogarth Press (1914) pp. 37–48

81 'less pleasant characteristics' Bella Southorn letter, August 12, 1917 (S)

81 *Times Literary Supplement* T.L.S., October 15, 1914

82 'The war ... killed it dead' 3 LW 91

82 Leonard's total earnings LW diary for 1914. His earnings from books were £46 8s. 1d. in 1914, £102 7s. 0d. in 1915

82 'could compel a steam roller' VW letter 672 (May 28, 1913)

83 'In December 1918' *The Times*, August 21, 1969

83 'every secret of a writer's soul' *Orlando*, pp. 189–90

83n 'Mr L. S. Woolf ... has collated' copy of *International Government* owned by one of the authors.

84 The *T.L.S.* reviewer T.L.S., April 1, 1915

84 Two Harley Street doctors Letters from Doctors Craig and Wright, May 10 and 19, 1916 (S)

90 'Leonard has been completely exempted' VW letter 770 (June 25, 1916)

90 had shrunk to less than half Income tax certificates dated May 22, 1919, May 31, 1921 and April 29, 1922 (S)

90 We also know that at least in 1918 VW letters, 915, 940

90 'never worried' about money   3 LW 91, 93

90 Virginia had stated   VW letter 631 (June 24, 1912)

94 they were furious with Virginia   VW letter 1182 (June 1921)

94 'A humorous sort of tenderness'   *Night and Day*, p. 107

94 'only a story one makes up'   *Night and Day*, p. 265

94 'You've destroyed my loneliness'   *Night and Day*, p. 534

94 The reviewer for the *Times Literary Supplement*   *T.L.S.*, October 30, 1919

94 Philip Noel-Baker said   *The Times*, August 21, 1969

94 When asked to sugar-coat this   Hamilton Holt correspondence, 1922 (S)

94 'It is love that alone'   *Essays on Life, Art and Science* (1908) p. 36

97 The *Times Literary Supplement*   *T.L.S.*, October 26, 1922

97 'This time the reviews'   AWD 54

CHAPTER 7: THE HOGARTH PRESS

The figures in this chapter, except where otherwise noted, were derived from a bound accounts book maintained by Leonard Woolf (1) for his personal affairs through 1912 (pages 1–87) and (2) for the operations of The Hogarth Press from 1917 to 1923–4 (pages 88 to 190). This accounts book, now on deposit in the University of Sussex Library, is herein referred to as 'Acct Bk'. Transactions subsequent to 1923–4 were entered in another book which has not been found.

page

99   £19   Acct Bk 89

99   pamphlet at 1s. 6d. (and information that follows down to next note) Acct Bk 94, 96–7; the original intention had been to offer the pamphlet at 1s. 2d. See 2 QB 41

100   the Press cleared £6 7s.   This is the profit through the end of 1917; another 14s. profit was accumulated through 1919. Acct Bk 90, 94

101   £2 2s. 6d.   Acct Bk 93, 102. See Barbara Bagenal letter, May 17, 1967 (S): 'My share of the profits was 2/6'

101   Priced at 3s. 6d.   Acct Bk 101–2

101   The author's royalties   Acct Bk 94, 132

101   Hogarth profit   Acct Bk 90, 88, 132

101   Cecil's poems   Printed in March 1918 and probably distributed then, although not noticed in the *T.L.S.* until January 23, 1919

102   'Mr Eliot . . . is an American'   VW letter 1044 (May 8, 1919)

102   'Middleton Murry edits the *Athenaeum*'   VW letter 1044 (May 8, 1919)

103   'the best-hated man'   *Dictionary of National Biography*, OUP (1951–60) p. 761

103   'Murry and Eliot ordered, and not me'   AWD 14 (May 12, 1919)

103   42 copies of *Kew Gardens* had been sold   Acct Bk 111

103   Eliot's sales were 33 and Murry's 27   Acct Bk 107 and 109

104   'the hall table stacked'   AWD 15 (June 10, 1919)

104   'as much praise was allowed'   AWD 15 (June 10, 1919)

CHAPTER 8: CAREERS: YEARS OF TRIUMPH

(Annual earnings of Leonard, Virginia and Hogarth Press taken from LW diaries for the several years).

116 Virginia said it meant *nothing* VW letter to Roger Fry, May 27, 1927 (S)

116 'a little fiction mixed with fact' 'The New Biography', 4 *Essays* p. 233

117 At one point (and quotations following) *Orlando* (1928) pp. 243, 181, 172

117 In 1928 Virginia was asked AWD 123; *A Room of One's Own* p. 5 fn

117 The masculine meal (and quotations following) *A Room of One's Own* pp. 16–17, 27, 158

118 In 1929 Virginia's royalties 4 LW 142

118 a quarter of his time 5 LW 99

118 Russell Sedgwick *Time and Tide*, October 17, 1931

119 The *Times Literary Supplement* T.L.S., October 22, 1931

119 'The sea is a miracle' VW letter 407 (April 20, 1908)

119 'all about nothing' 2 QB 162 citing AWD (B) September 15, 1931

119 'one of the three greatest English novels' *The Listener*, October 10, 1968

119 'there are very few authorities' *Flush* (1933) p. 151

120 'sick to death of it' VW letter to Philippa Woolf, September 29, 1939 (Sc)

120 In 1935, for example AWD 243

121 Violent transatlantic pressures Letter Christabel Aberconway to VW, September 12, 1940 (S); letter, Octavia Wilberforce to Elizabeth Robins, December 23, 1940 (S)

121 Leonard believed that the ultimate aims *Barbarians at the Gate*, Gollancz (1939) pp. 61–3, 70, 73, 190–3

121 'So far as the control and use of power goes' *Barbarians at the Gate* pp. 181–2

123 Eliot thought it her best novel Stephen Spender letter, July 2, 1953 (S)

123 'The Russian Point of View' *The Common Reader* (1925) pp. 219, 223, 224–5

CHAPTER 9: OLD FRIENDS AND NEW

page

125 'vanished like the morning mist' VW letter 746 (March 19, 1916)

125 'It is so long' AWD 12

126 'that Mr Grant' 1 QB 128–9

127 'I seldom see Lytton' 2 QB 155 from AWD (B) September 2, 1930

127 'we were all rather nice' Sydney-Turner letter to VW, February 9, 1919 (S)

128 'who, if he has the face of a pig' LW letter to Strachey, November 4, 1906 (S)

128 'I detest Keynes' LW letter to Strachey, October 23, 1908 (S)

128 Virginia regarded VW letter 1082 (September 14, 1919)

128 'a curious mixture' E. M. Forster letter, May 15, 1923 (S)

128 'I have always liked Maynard' Kingsley Martin letter, July 6, 1945 (S)

128 'his attempts to keep' VW letter 770 (June 25, 1916)

128 'a most shifty and wormy character' Michael Holroyd, *Lytton Strachey*, Heinemann (1968) vol. 2, p. 70

128 '90% of him' LW Letter to Quentin Bell, December 1, 1966 (S)

128 'could be the most entrancing' *New Statesman*, October 6, 1967, p. 438

128 'would display' *New Statesman*, January 30, 1932, p. 119

128 'amused affection' *The Times*, November 13, 1962

128 'He upset the ink' VW letter 499 (August 7, 1909)

130 'actually devastate me' Sydney Waterlow letter, January 18, 1942 (S)

130 On at least one occasion Conversation with Barbara Bagenal, 1975

130 'amounted almost to genius' LW in *The Listener*, March 26, 1953

130 'Desmond has an abnormal power' AWD 77–8

130 'He has a simple rather sunny nature' Undated LW MS–'Aspasia' paper (S)

130 Roger Fry claimed Roger Fry letter, September 13, 1924 (S)

130 'cockatoo' VW letter 903 (January 17, 1918)

130 'little hop o' my thumb' VW letter 1201 (November 2, 1921)

130 'all bottom and a little flaxen wig' VW letter 1215 (February 11, 1922)

130 'No one felt more seriously' 1 *Essays*, 356, 357

130 'Pray consider' Katherine Mansfield letter to VW, undated, from 141A Church St, Chelsea (S)

134 'mud-coloured and mute' AWD 12

134 'a posturing Byronic little man' VW letter 1228 (March 20, 1922)

134 'a bit "haunted"' by Virginia Katherine Mansfield letter undated, from 141A Church St., Chelsea (S)

134 Twenty years after they parted AWD 363

134 never shaved Robert Sencourt, *T. S. Eliot A Memoir*, Garnstone Press (1971) p. 68, see also 4 LW 109

134 out for a country walk 4 LW 108

134 'The critics say' 4 LW 111

134 Possum now wishes Berg

135 'a guards' officer' LW letter to Molly MacCarthy, October 2, 1924 (S)

135 'pen of brass' VW letter to Jacques Raverat, December 26, 1924 (S)

135 Virginia felt as a lover feels' 2 QB 117

135 There may have been' 2 QB 119

135 'I love Virginia' Nigel Nicolson, *Portrait of a Marriage*, Weidenfeld & Nicolson (1973) p. 203–4

143 'The physical element' *ibid*, p. 205

143 1927 (B)

143 'On the 24th the Nicolsons' Vanessa Bell to VW, April 27, 1935 (S)

143 'got up to look' VW letter 978 (October 12, 1918)

143 'the Prime Minister and half the Cabinet' 4 LW 105
    Lady Cunard *Emerald and Nancy*, Daphne Fielding (1968)

143 'loving to cut a dash' Christopher St John, *Ethel Smyth a Biography*, Longmans (1959) p. 223

143n '... it's a great thing' VW letter to Vita Sackville-West, January 31,

144 He thought Lady Colefax VW letter to Janet Case, July 7, 1937 (S)

144 'What a deal of cold business' *Essays on Literature, History, Politics, etc.* (1927) p. 13

CHAPTER 10: MALICE OR MISCHIEF?

page
145 Virginia's purchase 2 QB 47
146 'as excited as a schoolgirl' Gerald Brenan, *South from Granada*, Hamish Hamilton (1957) p. 142
146 'sweet and childlike nature' *Portrait of a Marriage* (1973) p. 205
146 'was full of surprises' 2 QB 96
146 'As often as not' Aileen Pippett, *The Moth and the Star* (Boston, 1953) p. 180
146 I wish I could think VW letter to Hugh Walpole, July 16, 1930 (Sc)
146 'Go away Vita' Conversation with Nigel Nicolson, 1976
146 'Will you come with me' J. R. Noble, editor, *Recollections of Virginia Woolf by her Contemporaries* (1972) p. 153
147 'Yet even in this light' *Jacob's Room*, p. 217
147 This letter was signed 'Thomas Gage' letter, December 12, 1922 (S)
148 she combined in a play MH/A256 (S)
148 they were Lytton Strachey and Dora Carrington VW letter 1340 (December 29, 1922)
149 dressed as Cupid Ronald Chapman, *The Laurel & the Thorn*, Faber (1945) p. 72
150 recently discovered diary Gladys Easdale, U. London Library MS 656/4
151 'merciless chaff' Dora Sanger letter March 6, [1930?] (S) yet this letter clearly suggests that Dora Sanger took the 'cruelty' as a joke
151 'tell Virginia' Barbara Rothschild letter, n.d. (S)
151 'I wish one day you would write' VW letter to Dorothy Bussy, September 3, 1930, offered in 1964 catalogue of Alan G. Thomas, bookseller, 7(a) Wimborne Road, Bournemouth
152 'stinks like a ... civet cat' 2 QB 45 from AWD(B) October 11, 1917

CHAPTER 11: THE PRIOR OF LEWES

page
153 'If I wanted some one' James Bartholomew letter, October 20, 1963 or 1964 (S)
154 'He was a strict Jew' VW letter 748 (March 27, 1916)
154 in a heated exchange with the Archbishop LW letter to Lord Fisher of Lambeth, April 1, 1968 (S)
154 'We are Jews' VW letter to Margaret Llewelyn Davies, April 28, 1935 (S)
154 Leonard declared LW letter to Dan Jacobson, June 3, 1968 (S)
154 Leonard ... failed to give adequate credit Bella Southorn letter, November 21, 1959 (S)
154 'You gave no weight' Philip Woolf letter, December 4, 1953 (S)
154 'I feel passionately' 5 LW 166-7
155 'Ever since I began to take any part in politics' LW letter to Gore Graham, November 17, 1937 (S)

155 'I admire and sympathize' LW letter to Lyn Newman, August 1, 1957 (S)

155 Beatrice Webb describes *Beatrice Webb's Diaries 1924–1932*, Longmans (1956) p. 131

155 'could not understand' 1 LW 46

155 'I could, if pushed' 1 LW 52

155n Leonard claimed 1 LW 50

156 'I think T. S. Eliot' LW letter to Michael Goldman, August 30, 1967 (S)

156 'In conversation and every day life' LW letter to Lyall Wilkes, January 13, 1968 (S)

156 she was bitterly attacked *New Statesman*, September 18, 1937

156 he subsequently expressed regret LW letter to H. M. Swanwick, September 29, 1937 (S)

156 a review he wrote *Political Quarterly*, vol. 33 (1962) pp. 228–9

156 'I ought not to have reviewed' LW letter to Margaret Cole, July 5, 1962 (S)

157 a review by Leonard *The Listener*, January 25, 1951

157 Harrod expressed R. F. Harrod letter, August 31, 1960 (S)

157 'I ought never to have reviewed' LW letter to R. F. Harrod, September 2, 1960 (S)

157 the advice he had given others LW letter to Richard Aldington, August 27, 1925 (S)

157 Leonard's self-conscious creation 1 LW 71

157 'I claim to be more serious' LW letter to Lyn Newman, July 5, 1957 (S)

158 'It was useless to argue with him' J. M. Keynes, *Two Memoirs* (1949) p. 85

158 The reviewer of *Quack, Quack!* *The Listener*, June 26, 1935

158 found Leonard courteous and charming Conversation, Angus Davidson, 1975

158 'a dyed in the wool Woolf' LW letter to Cecil Woolf, August 28, 1968 (S)

158 If you read old numbers of *Punch* *Essays on Literature, History, Politics, etc* (1927) p. 86

159 'I am glad you take my advice' LW letter to Gillian Tulip (1965) (S)

159 'pruned trees and my finger' LW Diary for December 30, 1919

159 'remarkable for his great courage' *Political Quarterly* 1967, p. 315

159 'Rudyard Kipling was a genius' LW MS (S)

159 'I acquired an affection' LW MS: 'The Prehistoric New Statesman and Nation' (S)

159 'Kingsley's mind' *Political Quarterly*, 1969, pp. 241, 242

159 If chalk for cement works LW letter to E. Sussex County Council, March 24, 1968 (S)

159 'I hope your use of the word nest' LW letter to John Lehmann, October 19, 1967 (S)

160 'pretty, lively, sweet-natured' 2 LW 102

160 'it so happens' LW letter to Lytton Strachey, November 17, 1907 (S)

160 The position is this   LW letter to John Lehmann, September 18, 1943 (S)

160 'At one of my meetings'   Noel Annan, *Leslie Stephen*, MacGibbon & Kee (1951) p. 270

CHAPTER 12: THE HOMEMAKERS

page
162 cook her wedding ring   VW letter 714 (December 10, 1914)

162 'my books run to about 17s. a head   VW letter 824 (February 11, 1917)

162 pinned together by brooches   VW letter 923 (April 22, 1918)

162 Bob Trevelyan burned out the seat of his trousers   LW MS written as foreword to letters of C. P. Trevelyan (S)

162 'Oh Leonard, look!'   Conversation, Rose Schrager, 1974

162 'Lottie and Leonard'   VW letter 980 (October 19, 1918)

162 'wild ass'   VW letter 1079 (September 9, 1919)

162 'intoxicated Jay'   VW letter 1196 (October 17, 1921)

162 'perfectly angelic'   VW letter 1335 (December 22, 1922)

162 'long letters, from friend to friend'   VW letter 1249 (May 18, 1922)

162 'she made a mouse'   VW letter 1336 (December 25, 1922)

162 Nellie had problems with her teeth   VW letter 1145 (September 12, 1920)

162 she was run over by a car   VW letter 1196 (October 17, 1921)

163 'an enchanted world'   VW letter 1099 (November 27, 1919)

163 the outcome of every game   LW diaries 1935–40

163 diary for June 22, 1940   AWD 336–7

164 'Leonard says we owe a great deal to Shaw'   VW letter 1250 (May 21, 1922)

164 they settled the issue   LW handwritten accounting (S)

164 personal 'hoard'   4 LW 142

164 Leonard's diary   Monks House diary (S)

172 'We travel with a selection of our books'   VW letter to Jacques Raverat July 30, 1923 (Sc)

172 The cost of maintaining two houses (and following figures on expenditures)   LW diaries 1917–40

173 'For years I never had a pound extra'   2 QB 155 from AWD (B) September 2, 1930

174 'my rooms are all vast panels'   VW letter to Janet Case, April 12, 1924 (S)

174 the 'old umbrella'   Conversation with Angus Davidson, 1975

174 'Woolf has been spuddling'   conversation with James Bartholomew, 1970

175 she occasionally borrowed things   VW letter 970 (September 12, 1918)

175 'I've had an accident'   VW leter 1202 (November 8, 1921)

175 'I can't forever appear'   VW letter 1321 (November 13, 1922)

175 Raymond Mortimer   The *Sunday Times*, September 21, 1975, p. 41

175 'as a weevil … eats cheese'   VW letter 1268 (August 10, 1922)

175 an 'incredible muddle'   *Harold Nicolson Diaries and Letters 1939–1945*, Collins (1967) p. 146

175 'further crowded by tin dishes' ibid., 147
176 'I daresay' 2 QB 71 from AWD (B) December 28, 1919
176 'I couldn't have married anyone else' VW letter 1280 (August 25, 1922)
176 'I owe all the happiness' 2 QB 226
176 'destroyed' her loneliness *Night and Day* (1919) p 534
176 'never pretend' 2 QB 89 from AWD (B) January 3, 1923; see also AWD 29
176n 'Saxon ... talked a great deal' VW letter 887 (October 30, 1917)
177 'the wisest decision' 1 QB 187
177 Thereafter they lived 'chastely' Conversation with Gerald Brenan, 1970
177 'poor Billy' VW letter to Vanessa Bell, July 23, 1927 (B)
177 'could not dispel a virginity' *Mrs Dalloway* (1925) p. 49
177 discussed at some length in Quentin Bell's biography 1 QB 42, 43, 61, 95, 96 – all relating to George Duckworth. Virginia also mentioned such an incident involving Gerald Duckworth MH/A5 p. 6 (S) Octavia Wilberforce writing about a conversation she had with Virginia in March 1941 reported: 'her stepbrother George D. she evidently adored'. Letter to Elizabeth Robins, March 14, 1941 (S)

CHAPTER 13: MONKS HOUSE EXILES

page
180 Leonard was able to skate LW diary for 1939 and 1940
180 'hated to feel cold' Louie Mayer in *Recollections of Virginia Woolf by her Contemporaries*, edited by J. R. Noble (1972) p. 159
180 'the wind cuts like a scythe' AWD 326 (February 9, 1940)
180 'The house is damp' AWD 364 (January 26, 1941)
180 'so still, so alert' Christopher St John, *Ethel Smyth, A Biography* (1959) p. 224
180 she kept the servants laughing 2 QB 53
180 Leonard's pet marmoset Conversation with Philippa Woolf Hardman, 1976
181 A Messerschmitt shot down AWD 354 (October 2, 1940)
181 'They came very close' AWD 342 (August 16, 1940)
181 'Eight of my city churches destroyed' AWD 362 (January 1, 1941)
181 'the desolate ruins of my old squares' AWD 363 (January 15, 1941)
181 'A strong feeling of invasion in the air' AWD 348 (September 13, 1940)
181 'Capitulation will mean All Jews to be given up' AWD 336 (June 9, 1940)
181 'for suicide should Hitler win' AWD 332 (May 13, 1940)
181 'I can't conceive ... that there will be a 27th June 1941' AWD 337 (June 22, 1940)
181 'How one enjoys food now' AWD 361 (December 29, 1940)
182 how agents of J. P. Morgan Letter Octavia Wilberforce to Elizabeth Robins, December 23, 1940 (S)
182 'had been sorting papers' *ibid.*

182 'irreparable blows' Letter Octavia Wilberforce to Elizabeth Robins, March 14, 1941 (S)

182 'She so actively both loved and hated' Letter Octavia Wilberforce to Elizabeth Robins, December 23, 1940 (S)

183 'looks a better colour' Letter Octavia Wilberforce to Elizabeth Robins, February 28, 1941 (S)

183 'feeling desperate' Letter, Octavia Wilberforce to Elizabeth Robins, March 14, 1941 (S)

183 'During part of the last war' *ibid.*

183 *Orlando* and her book on Fry, were 'failures' Letter Octavia Wilberforce to Elizabeth Robins, March 22, 1941 (S)

183 'What shall we do' Letter Vanessa Bell to VW, March 20, 1941 (S)

183 The interview was difficult' 2 QB 225–6
They said: 'Come to tea & let us comfort you' LW undated MS (S)

CHAPTER 14: AN EPILOGUE

page

187 a letter from the Prime Minister Letter from Harold Wilson, May 6, 1966 (S)

187 Leonard said LW letter to Prime Minister Harold Wilson, May 11, 1966 (S)

188 'purple tweeds' Andreas Mayor letter, November 26, 1966 (S)

NOTE ON ABBREVIATIONS

In our system of notation, 'LW' stands for Leonard, 'VW' for Virginia. The five volumes of Leonard's autobiography are referred to as 'LW' with a prefix to indicate the number of the volume and a suffix to indicate the page. The two volumes of Quentin Bell's biography are referred to as 'QB' with a similar indication of volume and page. The four volumes of *Collected Essays* by Virginia Woolf, published in 1966 and 1967 (The Hogarth Press), are cited as 'Essays'. The initials 'AWD' have been used for *A Writer's Diary, being Extracts from the Diary of Virginia Woolf, edited by Leonard Woolf* (1953), except that 'AWD(B)' refers to the original diaries of Virginia Woolf held by the Berg. The phrase 'VW letter' followed by a number refers to the numbering system adopted by Nigel Nicolson in the volumes of Virginia Woolf letters edited by him. In the case of letters received by Leonard, only the name of the writer of the letter and its date, if known are given in the note. Materials in the University of Sussex are identified by the notation '(S)' or '(Sc)' if the Sussex copy is not the original or, in the case of letters written by Leonard, is not the carbon copy of the original; those at the Berg are identified by '(B)'.

INDEX